A River Flowed from Eden

A River
Flowed
from Eden

Torah for the
Shabbat Table

Rabbi Ari D. Kahn

KODESH PRESS

A River Flowed from Eden
© Ari D. Kahn, 2015
ISBN: 978-0692445303

Cover Art Courtesy of Ofra Friedland
www.ofrafriedland.co.il

Published & Distributed by

Kodesh Press L.L.C.
New York, NY
www.KodeshPress.com
kodeshpress@gmail.com

This volume is dedicated to

Mitchell R. Julis

On the occasion of his 60th birthday,
and in anticipation of the next 60 years.
May you be blessed with years of fulfillment
and days filled with laughter love and joy.

Table of Contents

Sefer Bereishit

Sefer Shemot

Sefer Vayikra

Sefer B'midbar

Sefer Devarim

Introduction

When I first began writing essays on the weekly *parashah* many years ago, some of my readers found them "long-winded" and encouraged me to subject my work to severe editing if I hoped to gain a wider readership. I resisted. It was my firm belief that there is no shortage of "Torah sound bites"; I preferred to be thorough rather than popular.

A few years ago, my close friend Mitch Julis asked me to write new, current, topical short essays on the weekly Torah portion. As is his wont, Mitch presented a compelling and well-conceived vision for this project. The present volume is a result of his vision.

Each week, as I set about composing my thoughts into a short essay, I consciously kept my intended audience in mind: people like Mitch and those to whom he might forward an email on a Friday morning to share an idea that might spark discussion at the Shabbat table. Until that point, I had addressed my writings to other teachers, eager students or Torah scholars. Now, I shifted the discussion so that it would include those whose work schedule or other responsibilities left them far less time to delve into the depths of the weekly Torah reading, but nonetheless sought an uplifting and challenging idea they could share with family and friends around the table on Friday night.

With this readership in mind, the tone and subject matter also evolved: These essays (originally called "the Echoes of Eden Project") became more personal, more contemplative and less didactic. These were essays that had to fit well with good food and wine, essays that could meld with the glowing backdrop of Shabbat candles and the gathering of the entire family—people of different ages, viewpoints and interests.

It is therefore particularly apt that this volume is dedicated to Mitch on the occasion of his 60th birthday: If not for his vision and encouragement, this project would not have come to fruition. May God grant him continued health, success and vigor. May Mitch and his wife Joleen know great joy and *nahat* from their wonderful family, and may those of us who cherish their friendship continue to take pleasure in their company and companionship for many years to come.

Along with Mitch and Joleen Julis, I would like to thank Raymond and Elizabeth Gindi for their continued support for all of my projects. May God bless them with good health and happiness and continued *nahat* from their children and grandchildren.

I would also like to thank Avraham and Sarah Manricks and Gabriel Manricks for creating rabbiarikahn.com, where these essays were originally posted each week. My thanks also to Alec Goldstein of Kodesh Press for his dedication and professionalism in producing this beautifully crafted book. Special thanks go to one of my most dedicated students, Rabbi Yoel Saidian, for making the introduction to Kodesh Press.

I would also like to thank the incomparable Ofra Freidland for allowing her beautiful artwork to adorn this volume.

Most of all I thank my wife, collaborator, editor and partner Naomi for her skill and love in turning the words of a clumsy yeshiva student into elegant prose.

Ari Kahn
18 Iyar 5775 – 33rd Day of the Omer
הוד שבהוד
Givat Ze'ev

ספר
בראשית

Parashat Bereishit
Working and Guarding

The first *parashah* in the Book of *Bereishit* may be the most challenging and difficult of all sections of the Torah. The verses that describe the unfolding of the creation of the universe are cloaked in mystery and laden with allusion. And yet, though the language of the verses is difficult and the ideas sublime, we sense that this *parashah* contains the key to understanding the very foundation of all existence.

Strangely enough, perhaps the single greatest mystery of all, the question that has occupied mankind's intellect and imagination since the very dawn of life, is actually very clearly and simply answered in this *parashah*: What is the purpose of our existence? Why did God create us? Why are we here? This existential dilemma has tortured and tantalized man since the day of his creation, but the Torah makes short work of it in *Bereishit*, preempting the question with a relatively clear, albeit brief statement that is therefore easily overlooked.

> God took the man and placed him in the Garden
> of Eden to work it and guard it (*Bereishit* 2:15).

This statement is surely not as exciting as a talking serpent, nor as enticing as the luscious fruit of a certain tree, yet it lays out the mandate for all human endeavor with two simple words: working and guarding. As the Torah continues, more commandments will be added in order to flesh out this mandate and give humankind the tools to fulfill it. In fact, the very next verse contains critical information, in language that may be considered a commandment, regarding the trees of the Garden, specifically which trees may be enjoyed and which must be avoided. The ensuing books of the Torah add more and more commandments, some for all of mankind and others exclusively for the Jewish People, yet all of the commandments may very well fit into these two primordial categories: "working" and "guarding."

Let us consider these categories and the dynamic each sets in motion: "Working" implies forward movement, expansion, while "guarding" implies the creation of boundaries, of containment. These two gestures are not mutually exclusive; quite the opposite, they represent two sides of the same coin, a type of "yin and yang," opposites that balance one another and create a sustainable existence. This is what my revered teacher, Rabbi Yosef Dov Soloveitchik, referred to as an unresolved Hegelian dialectic, in which thesis and antithesis can—and indeed must—coexist without melting into a synthesis.

The course of human history may be seen as an expression of man's basic attempts to subdue and harness nature for his needs; this expansive urge is the "work" we do. But what of protecting nature? Can we similarly describe human history as the ongoing search for balance, as the quest to preserve the resources at our disposal, to preserve and renew the world in which we live? Has human history tended far more to be a story of scorched earth policy in which the work of human progress ignores the commandment to protect the Garden, for our own protection? Has human history repeatedly been the story of the man who kills the goose that lays the proverbial golden eggs?

"Scorched earth" is a concept borrowed from military jargon, describing a policy employed by a conquering force bent on decimating the opposing side. This policy is born of a particular breed of tunnel vision in which the end justifies the means and all casualties are seen as unavoidable collateral damage. No thought is given to the realities that will exist at the end of the war; no consideration is given to the viability of life in the conquered territory. Fundamentally, the conqueror sees himself as inflicting damage on his foe, and not on himself. The land he leaves in his wake, the scorched and uninhabitable earth, is not his own. It belongs to someone else—someone for whom he has no responsibility. Were the conqueror to consider that the people whose lands he lays to waste will soon become his own subjects, and their sustenance and welfare will soon become his responsibility, there would be no sense inflicting wanton destruction. Much like the owner of the golden goose, he allows short-term considerations to blind him to long-term needs.

This is the message contained in the brief statement in *Bereishit* that describes the human mandate as equal parts of "to work" and "to protect": The seemingly unstoppable steamroller of human accomplishment should not come at the cost of a swath of destruction left in its wake. The earth we scorch is the source of our own sustenance; the "golden goose" is the key to our own future survival. We have been entrusted with the task of tending and guarding the natural resources that sustain us; they are our responsibility, and our forward progress is both impossible and meaningless without them.

However, the message of *Bereishit* is even more profound. Man is given a creative role, a unique ability, above all other creatures, to enter into a partnership in creation—as junior partners, to be sure, but partners nonetheless. We are entrusted beyond the role of watchman over someone else's assets; we are commanded to expand and grow those assets, to improve the partnership's holdings, to explore and take a degree of control over the partnership's resources, for our own benefit. Because we are partners with God in this venture, there is holiness in productivity as well as holiness in sustainability. "To work" and "to protect" are both expressions of our ongoing involvement in the partnership with the Divine.

Where have we gone wrong? What was true in the Garden of Eden is equally true today: Man turns his back on the partnership, convinces himself that he is sole owner of the assets and that the rules of the partnership are not binding. As in Eden, the result is alienation, dissolution, exile. Our failure to curb our desires, our failure to balance our urge to expand with our urge to protect, has laid the garden to waste. We leave behind scorched earth and slain golden geese. To find our way back to the garden, we must rekindle the partnership and recommit to its founding principle, the balance with which we were charged from the very outset: To work and to protect.

Parashat Noach
The Terrible Secret of the Tower

The story of the Tower of Babel is well known: Mankind unites to build an edifice that will reach the heavens. God descends and frustrates the plan; man is dispersed, and a language barrier, not a tower, is erected.

> The entire earth had one language with uniform words. When [the people] migrated from the east, they found a valley in the land of Shinar, and they settled there. They said to one another, "Come, let us mold bricks and fire them." They then had bricks to use as stone, and clay for mortar. They said, "Come, let us build ourselves a city, and a tower whose top shall reach the sky. Let us make ourselves a name, so that we will not be scattered over the face of the earth" (*Bereishit* 11:1-3).

The text of the Torah is terse; while we are told that they gather in a valley, and build a city and tower, more words are used to describe the actual construction than any other aspect of the story. The gathering of the raw materials, and turning earth into bricks and bricks into a structure, make up the bulk of the text.[1]

We are not told why God deemed it necessary to halt the project, although rabbinic sources reveal that there was

---

1. See Malbim *Bereishit* 11:1, Rabbenu Bachya *Bereishit* 11:4, *Pardes Yosef, Bereishit* 11:1, *Ha'amek Davar, Bereishit* 11:3.

something so heinous about this plan that the record of the entire episode was censored and its shocking details suppressed.[2]

In order to unveil the dark heart of this episode that lies behind the terse language of the text, we must first ask a basic, obvious question regarding the scant information we have been given: If the plan was to reach heaven—perhaps to "declare war" on God, as some scholars[3] have suggested, why build in the low terrain of the valley and not on a mountain?[4] If the plan was to prevent the destruction of a future flood, again—why not build on higher ground? Furthermore, building on a mountain would surely have simplified the process and enhanced the results: Quarrying stone would have been far more effective than making bricks. Why, then, gather in a valley and suffer these disadvantageous conditions?

Traditional sources provide us with a small but crucial bit of information. This valley was the lowest area, and it became the drainage route for the waters of the flood. The ecosystem in this valley was comprised of the debris from the flood.

The shocking implication is that the new tower was built using the physical remains of the previous generation. The bricks were made from the sediment in the valley—sediment created when an entire generation was eradicated.[5]

---

2. *Bereishit Rabbah* 38:6.

3. *Targum Yonatan*, *Bereishit* 11:4.

4. See *Gur Aryeh*, *Bereishit* 11:1.

5. *Midrash Aggadah* 11:2, Jerusalem Talmud, *Berachot* 4:1 (7b), *Bereishit Rabbah* 37:4, Talmud Bavli, *Berachot* 57b, Talmud Bavli *Shabbat* 113b, Rashi *Berachot* 57b, s.v. *makom*.

פירוש קדמון מבית מדרשו של ר' פרחיה (בשיטת הקדמונים) מסכת שבת קיג:

ואמרינן בגמרא האוכל מעפר בבל כאילו אוכל מעצמות אבותיו. שלא נקרא שמה שנער אלא משום שננערו כל מיתי המבול לשם:

What motivated them to create their tower on these foundations? Here, we must proceed with caution. Apparently, the new generation had developed some type of animosity towards a God whom they perceived as merciless and destructive. Careful consideration of what is not in the text shows that God is not part of their narrative; this is why some scholars have characterized their cause as a "war against Heaven." Perhaps they saw the tower as a type of memorial for the victims, made out of the very victims it was intended to memorialize. Alternatively, their behavior may have been no more than callous disregard. Infatuated with their new technology, history held no interest for this generation. Stories of the past were of no consequence, and they concerned themselves only with progress and the future.

Other rabbinic traditions take on a new light when considered through the prism of this gruesome episode: Elsewhere, our sages recount that our patriarch Avraham was thrown into the furnace when he expressed belief in one God. The very same furnace used to create these ghoulish bricks was meant to quell Avraham's voice of dissent. While the text emphasizes the positive trait of unity displayed in the building of the tower, their unity was apparently achieved through brutal enforcement. This society was intolerant of dissenting opinions. Sadly, human history has proven more than once that it is a very short leap between turning one's back on the past, to (literally or figuratively) misusing the remains of the dead, to killing those who disagree with you.

The generation of the tower, unified in trampling upon the remains of the previous generation as well as the rights of dissenters amongst them, was fated to lose the unity which they abused.

As for us, we prefer Avraham—who emerges unscathed from the furnace, committed to decency and kindness. We reject the voice of the mob, the united but tyrannical masses who trampled their fellow man and desecrated the remains of those who came before them in order to build an edifice they believed would bring them honor and glory.

Parashat Lech Lecha
Deconstructing and Reconstructing Avraham

In Jewish tradition, Avraham is seen as the archetype of *hesed*[6]; he is known not merely as the best example of loving kindness, but as the mortal reflection of this attribute of God. *Hesed* is often understood as "giving," and Avraham's reputation is built largely on the Torah's description of his enthusiasm in catering to the needs of his guests. Rabbinic tradition adds even more details of Avraham's yearning to perform acts of kindness and his eager anticipation of wayward travelers.

These sources notwithstanding, a closer look at some of the other details of Avraham's biography recorded in the Torah paints a portrait that may seem incongruous with the trait of *hesed*.

First, Avraham deserts his elderly father; he puts his wife in a precarious situation—not once but twice. He parts ways with his orphaned nephew Lot, whom he had once considered his own heir. He becomes embroiled in regional conflicts and goes to war. He capitulates to Sarah's demands and banishes his maid, whom he has impregnated. Later he casts her, and their child, out of his house. He performs circumcision on his entire household. Even when he negotiates with God to save the city of Sodom, he does not seek mercy for the sinners. His argument

---

6. This idea is expressed in rabbinic sources. See, for example, *Bereishit Rabbah* 73:2.

is that it would be improper to kill the righteous along with the wicked. Last but certainly not least, he is prepared to slaughter his own beloved son. While each of these episodes can and should be studied and analyzed, the sum total of his life's work may not appear to justify his reputation as "the man of *hesed*" *par excellence.* So many of his actions and reactions seem to be incongruous with the spirit of kindness.

How can we reconcile the Avraham that arises from these episodes with the traditional view of his character? Let us make a few suggestions:

We can postulate that at the core Avraham was, in fact, as kind as we have always been led to believe. The situations of conflict in which he so often found himself were not of his own choosing but rather were tests, designed to elevate him, to hone and clarify his personality and bring new facets to light.

Alternatively, or perhaps additionally, we may be forced to reconsider our understanding of *hesed* itself. What constitutes *hesed?* While we may judge actions or motivations, these do not always dovetail: Some acts that may seem kind may be motivated by something else altogether, and some kind intentions may have results that are far from kind. A case in point is Avraham's decision to go to war in order to free innocent captives. Here is an important moral lesson for those who see *hesed* as synonymous with non-violence and pacifism: The Torah definition of *hesed* is not that espoused by Gandhi, who advised the Jews to go as sheep to the slaughter and believed that fighting—even fighting Nazis—is immoral, just as any and every war is immoral. Avraham, the archetype of kindness, knew—and not in a theoretical sense—that at times one must fight for peace. When he fought to liberate Lot, both his motivation and the results of his actions were *hesed* even though the means used to achieve this goal may seem to us to be at odds with our own perception of what *hesed* means.

25

Perhaps a better description of Avraham's personality would be that he was deeply engaged and involved in the lives of others. He displayed, in every one of the episodes mentioned above, an overarching concern for the welfare of others. He sought to better the world—one person at a time. He was not content with his own personal insight, understanding, revelation; he did not seclude himself or disengage from those who did not share his worldview. In this, he stands in stark distinction to Noach, who, when told that destruction was at hand, that the impending storm would be catastrophic, did not reach out to others, did not raise his voice to God or his fellow man in protest or warning. Noah did not impact another living soul.

The Gemara[7] teaches that a real turning point for the world took place in the fifty-second year of Avraham's life. Born in the year 1948, Avraham was 52 years old when the new millennium arrived. Thus, the first 2000 years of human history are characterized as years of *tohu*—void, emptiness, self-absorption. From the year 2000, when Avraham began to teach his ideas, the years of revelation—Torah—began. This, then, is the real nature of the *hesed* of Avraham: His care for others, his deep engagement with the world around him, spurred him to share his insight, to teach and impact others with truth. The driving force of this *hesed* was the desire to fulfill the will of God; this may be seen as Avraham's *hesed*—*vis à vis* God Himself.

Our ability to discern the *hesed* in all the episodes of Avraham's biography often requires nuanced thinking, yet careful examination of Avraham's words and deeds can empower us to live his legacy of *hesed* toward our fellow man and toward our Creator. True *hesed* is not pacifism, nor is it moral relativism that seeks to attain peace at the expense of truth. *Hesed* can only be meaningful when it springs from the deep desire to emulate God's attributes and share God's blessings with others.

---

7. Talmud Bavli *Avodah Zarah* 9a.

Parashat Vayera
Practice What You Preach

Oh God said to Abraham, "Kill me a son"
Abe says, "Man, you must be puttin' me on"
— Bob Dylan, "Highway 61 Revisited"

The narrative of the Binding of Isaac, *Akeidat Yitzchak,* is introduced with one terse statement: "After these events, the Almighty tested Avraham." Unlike the protagonist in Bob Dylan's version, our patriarch Avraham does not engage God in conversation or argument, nor does he offer a (glib) rejoinder. He silently marches on to his cruel destiny. Perhaps Avraham's uncharacteristic silence indicates that he knew he was being tested. This leaves us with one glaring, yet often ignored question: What are "these events" that precipitated the test? What context could possibly shed light on *Akeidat Yitchak*?

In general, things were not easy for Avraham. As an island of monotheism in a sea of paganism, his life was complex and his interpersonal relationships often strained. In so many instances, not only was Avraham in mortal danger, his wife Sarah was caught in the crossfire. And yet, this Torah portion illustrates that Sarah was not merely a long-suffering partner in Avraham's wanderings and a stalwart supporter of her husband's cause. In more than one instance, Sarah was the focus of the conflict, the object of the carnal desires of others—including powerful monarchs who were accustomed to having their way. In these instances, Avraham had a pre-arranged cover story: He instructed his wife to play along with his claim that he and Sarah were siblings and not spouses. While this strategy saved Avraham on more than one occasion, it turned Sarah into a human shield of sorts (and created a moral quandary for us, the reader). Remarkably, Sarah escaped each of these difficult situations unscathed. Perhaps Avraham sensed that Sarah's holiness, or the Divine blessing he had received, would protect them both from the hostile world in which they lived.

One such powerful adversary was Avimelech. Upon Avraham's arrival in his domain, Avimelech sends his henchmen, who simply take Sarah to their leader—no questions asked, no courtship, no consent. That night, Avimelech receives a stern message in a dream: God informs him that his behavior renders him a "dead man." To save his life (and kingdom) he must return the woman to her husband.

In the morning, Avraham is summoned; Avimelech, furious at the deception, demands that Avraham explain himself. The dialogue is fascinating. Avimelech bellows: How could you have misled me, leading me to almost sleep with a married woman? Avimelech seems sincerely upset, and his moral outrage is poignantly conveyed in the text:

> Avimelech summoned Avraham and said to him, "How could you do this to us? What terrible thing did I do to you that you brought such great guilt upon me and my people? The thing you did to me is simply not done!" (*Bereishit* 20:9-10).

Avraham does not respond; perhaps he thinks the question is rhetorical. Yet Avimelech continues; he changes his tone and seems genuinely interested in learning something from Avraham:

> "What did you see that made you do such a thing?"
> (*Bereishit* 20:10).

At last, Avraham speaks. He explains that as Sarah's husband, his own life was in danger. While in his own mind Avimelech was a moral man who would never sleep with a married woman, his morality was skewed: If he found a desirable woman who was married, he would, without hesitation, kill the husband and "free" the widow. A married woman was off-limits, but murder was a normal part of the power structure of pagan society in which "might makes right." In one single, seemingly extraneous phrase, Avraham's response points out to Avimelech the absurdity of the pagan system of values:

> "The only thing lacking in this place is fear of God"
> (*Bereishit* 20:11).

This, Avraham explains, is the crux of his predicament: Avimelech is moral—but his morality is local and subjective. Avraham, on the other hand, lives by morality of a higher order, an objective morality whose source is God. In Avraham's system, God defines morality, and whatever God commands is, by definition, moral. Avraham attempts to impart this understanding to Avimelech, but we may imagine that his sermon fell on deaf ears.

It is in this context that Avraham is tested: When God calls upon him to offer up his son, Avraham finds himself in a self-created quandary. In his encounter with Avimelech, he had preached absolute morality based on fear of God. Now, God has commanded him to commit an act that may have seemed to him the antithesis of morality, of kindness, of every Divine attribute that Avraham had come to know and emulate. Could Avraham live up to the standards he had so recently demanded of others? Could he behave differently than Avimelech and his nation of pagans? Could he set aside his own subjective understanding of morality and obey the word of God unquestioningly?

As he marches forward, silently focused on his mission, Avraham proves that he is prepared to fear and obey God no matter what the cost, no matter what the task. As the knife in his hand descends toward his son's neck, the episode comes to an abrupt conclusion, as a heavenly voice calls out, "Now I know that you fear God"—not love God, not emulate God— but fear God. Now I know that you are willing to set aside your own subjective and limited human understanding and moral constructs in the face of God's commandments, as they represent absolute morality. Now I know that you practice what you preach.

This aspect of *Akeidat Yitzchak* is a frightening one, especially for rabbis and all those who preach to others: Beware when you preach, we are warned, for God may hold you to the same standards that you espouse. As in the case of Avraham's words to Avimelech, God just may call upon each and every one of us to practice what we preach. Let us hope that this lesson of *Akeidat Yitzchak* affects both what we preach, what we demand of others, as well as what we do to live up to the standards to which we hold our fellow man.

Parashat Hayei Sarah
Uncommon Decency

When the time arrives to find a bride for Yitzchak, Avraham sends his most trusted servant on a quest to find a suitable spouse. Those familiar with biblical courtships are not surprised that the fateful meeting takes place at a well; both Yaakov and Moshe meet their future wives at wells. And yet, despite the similarities, our present case differs from the others in several ways. The first difference is the most obvious: This case is the only instance of courtship by proxy. Additionally, Yaakov and Moshe demonstrated both physical and moral strength and won over the "damsel in distress," whereas in this case, Avraham's servant, identified as Eliezer, takes the opposite view. He creates a test; the first woman to pass it will be deemed suitable.

The test he puts in place is one of kindness and generosity: Will she offer water not only to a wayward traveler but to his parched camel as well? This is surely no arbitrary test: This servant of Avraham, raised in Avraham's holy tent, was privy to the inner workings of Avraham's mind, and he knew the significance of kindness within the hierarchy of his master's value system. Someone stingy or misanthropic could not be a part of Avraham's camp, certainly could not take on a leadership role, nor transmit Avraham's values to the next generation.

While in no way wishing to minimize the importance of decency and generosity, there seems to be a glaring omission from this test: What of her beliefs? What if the person who passed the test was a good-hearted polytheist? Could such a person really be chosen as a bride for the son of Avraham? Surely the nascent Jewish nation would need at its very core good deeds, generosity, sharing and giving, but if we know nothing else about Jewish thought, we know that all of these traits are seen as outgrowths of a highly developed sense of monotheism: The recognition that there is but one all-powerful God who has no needs leads to the realization that Creation was not designed to solve a problem or fulfill some need within God, but rather was an act of absolute altruism. Because God lacks nothing and is not affected by human behavior, because there is nothing humans can do for God, all we can do is attempt to emulate God and mimic His kindness. This realization was Avraham's contribution to the world, what set him apart from the society into which he was born, what informed his behavior and gave form and content to his life's work.

Was this what Eliezer was thinking? Did he see kindness as an expression of monotheism? Although we cannot know his motivations, one early commentator, Rabbenu Nissim,[8] suggested that Eliezer was in fact not at all concerned with the religious beliefs of the prospective bride. In fact, we may surmise that this aspect of her biography was not on the checklist at all: By sending an emissary back to his homeland, Avraham almost guaranteed that any bride Eliezer might find would be the product of an upbringing steeped in the idolatry that was standard fare in Mesopotamia. Avraham knew the place all too well: He had put quite a distance between himself and that culture, even prior to God's command to leave his family and birthplace. Surely, the prospective bride would have been raised and educated in that very same world, exposed to the same idols Avraham had smashed in his youth. What, then, was

---

8. *Derashot ha-Ran* 12.

Avraham's strategy in sending his servant there, of all places, and what was Eliezer thinking when he created his test?

Rabbenu Nissim suggests that when beliefs are compared with personality traits, the former are far easier to change than the latter. Presumably, as Avraham's *major domo*, his "right-hand man," Eliezer had seen people come and go. He saw how quickly and easily people changed their belief system, especially under Avraham's tutelage, yet he also saw how difficult it was for people to change personality traits. Even among Avraham's flesh and blood, poor character traits overshadowed religious belief; Lot and Yishmael both parted ways with Avraham's camp over differences that were not "religious" in nature. On the other hand, all four of our matriarchs were born and raised in Avraham's hometown, and all were from the same extended family of idol-worshippers, yet each of them rose above the value system in which they were raised, and exhibited the extraordinary character traits that are the core of Jewish ethics.

According to Rabbenu Nissim, Eliezer was confident that after spending time with Avraham, any idolater would become enlightened, would be liberated from polytheistic beliefs—but changing their character would be far more difficult. Simply put, teaching decency is far more difficult than teaching theology. This is not to say that is impossible for people to change their ways. Quite the opposite: this may be mankind's most important task—to change and elevate character traits. Yet when looking for a fitting spouse for Yitzchak, Eliezer chose decency over doctrine. In our generation, when common sense has become uncommon and common decency increasingly rare, the poignancy of this lesson should not be overlooked.

Parashat Toldot
Lessons of a Sale

Yitzchak and Rivka had two children, Esav and Yaakov. As twins, it goes without saying that they were extremely close in age. However, in a society in which the older child would have more responsibilities as well as greater privileges, those few minutes made a huge difference. And while questions of inheritance are often the cause of family strife, in the case of Yitzchak and Rivka's sons, the division of the estate was far more complicated. In this particular family, the inheritance at stake was not only financial. The legacy passed down from their grandfather, the patriarch Avraham, included a Divine promise that one day they would inherit the Land of Israel. However, this was far from a "no strings attached" arrangement. The path to this inheritance would involve years of exile and slavery.

The two sons, though they shared the same DNA and were raised in the same household, had very different personalities and outlooks. Esav was a man of immediate gratification. He focused on the here and now. To him, the offer of years of suffering and waiting for a reward sometime in the distant future was a cruel joke. The thought of waiting hundreds of years for his "payoff" was a painful absurdity. And so, when his brother Yaakov offered him something tangible and immediate in lieu of the birthright, Esav was delighted to take the "bargain." As far as he was concerned this was a "win-win" deal: He divested himself of an onerous burden and capitalized in the here-and-now in return from some vague and distant future benefit that was of questionable value. It is no coincidence that this section of the narrative ends with an editorial comment describing Esav's loathing for the birthright and the responsibility it entailed (*Bereishit* 25:34).

Yaakov, on the other hand, was more of a long-term thinker. He was willing to sacrifice the here-and-now, to postpone gratification for hundreds of years and accept almost unimaginable suffering, in order to acquire what he knew to be the family's true treasure: The Land of Israel. He justified his behavior by reminding himself that he had struck a deal that satisfied both sides: Esav got his soup and freed himself from responsibilities that did not interest him, and Yaakov got the Land of Israel—along with the price to be paid to inherit it.

And yet, even when we factor in the centuries of slavery in Egypt, the deal seems inequitable. We cannot help but contrast this transaction with Avraham's purchase of the first parcel of land in Israel: Despite the offer to receive the land as a gift, free of charge, Avraham insisted on paying full price, perhaps even an exorbitant price. Avraham understood that this purchase would have repercussions in the future, and he therefore made a point of paying the full asking price, and completing the deal in a publicly witnessed and fully legal and binding transaction. Somehow, we sense that Yaakov's business with Esav was not conducted in the same fashion. Despite Esav's satisfaction at the time, Yaakov may not have "paid in full"; perhaps additional payment for this "windfall" was still due.

As the narrative progresses, Yaakov establishes the major relationships that shape the rest of his life: First, the relationship with his boss/father-in-law, and by extension his wives; and second, the relationship with his children. His relationships all seem somehow strained, convoluted, troubled—and we cannot help but postulate that his own unresolved relationship with his brother lies at the root of his troubles. Yaakov switched places with his brother in the birthright episode, and later went so far as to disguise himself as Esav and take his place in line for their father's blessing. How surprised should he have been when his bride Rachel is replaced by her sister Leah? Even the most jaded reader who does not see the hand of God in history should appreciate the "karma" by which Yaakov is repaid with the very same behavior he himself used in his dealings with Esav.

Yaakov's relationships with his sons are no less complicated by his own past: First, Yaakov effectively switches places among his sons. Despite the order of their birth, Yaakov singles Yosef out, favors him above all the other sons, and treats him as if he were the firstborn. When Yaakov later loses Yosef and believes that he is dead, it is the result of another inequitable transaction: The brothers sell Yosef in exchange for a pair of shoes. Again, both sides are happy. Again, the brothers divest themselves of an unwanted burden. Again, immediate gratification obscures long-term responsibility.

Both in Yaakov's dealings with Esav and the brothers' dealings with Yosef, balance must be restored, the full price paid. Yaakov eventually inherits the Land of Israel, but years of suffering, exile and slavery were required to settle the account. Yosef eventually inherited a double portion in the Land of Israel, but he was the first of the brothers to be thrust into slavery, and he, like Yaakov, endured tremendous suffering, exile and alienation.

Man cannot shortchange God. Things we do to others come back to hurt and haunt us. Yaakov walked off with the birthright, and traded the Land of Israel for a bowl of soup. Unfortunately, it turned out to be a down-payment; the balance came due years later, in ways Yaakov never imagined.

Parashat Vayetzei
A Twice-Told Tale

The story seems strangely familiar: A band of Jews on the run, desperately trying to escape, wanting nothing more than to return to their ancestral homeland and live in peace. How many times throughout history has this story been repeated? The first time, the prototypical account, appears in *Parashat Vayetzei*: Yaakov and his family quit Lavan's house and start the journey home. Soon enough, Lavan gets word of what has happened and chases them down. Despite Yaakov's three-day head start, Lavan catches up with and confronts Yaakov on the seventh day. Words are exchanged, accusations fly. In the end, an understanding is reached and a covenant forged.

If the story seems familiar, perhaps it is because it was repeated many years later in the next book of the Torah. The Yaakov-Lavan story is the concise version of the great Exodus, yet although so many elements of the two stories are similar, there are enough differences to make us overlook the similarities. The most pronounced difference speaks to our tendency to think in terms of results rather than in terms of processes: In the Exodus story, there is no reconciliation, no understanding, no covenant. The hated Egyptians drown in the sea, in Divine retribution for the Jewish babies who suffered a similar plight.

Yet in terms of their structure, the two stories are strikingly similar. Both describe the escape, the almost-supernatural accrual of wealth, and the three-day chase culminating in confrontation on the seventh day. In fact, one of the greatest thinkers in Jewish history, Rabbi Eliyahu of Vilna, the famed Vilna Gaon, believed that these two accounts are actually the same story.[9] And yet, how far does this teaching attempt to take us? Was the Vilna Gaon referring to the stories' structure alone, or to the underlying message? Clearly, the Genius of Vilna could not have been referring to the conclusion of the story—or was he?

Looking beyond the superficial similarities of the two stories, we find that both the story of Yaakov's escape from Lavan and the story of the Jews' escape from Egypt involve more than physical exodus. Both stories are about leaving an alien culture and heading home. In both stories, the "hosts," the "other" side, who have benefited financially from the presence of the "stranger" in their midst, have strong reservations regarding the separation. Neither Lavan nor Pharaoh is willing to lose the benefits of having the Jews at their service.

But the Torah is not a book of history; it is a book of theology. The stories—especially those concerning our forefathers—are spiritual blueprints that affect all of Jewish history. The Exodus from Egypt unfolded as it did because of Yaakov's flight from the house of Lavan, and these two redemptions create the spiritual energy that will power the final redemption. Such is the secret of Jewish history: Time is cyclical, not linear. Throughout our history, events repeat themselves as the spiritual blueprint is expressed in different generations. For this reason, studying the past gives us insight into the present and the future.

In the case of redemption, we see before us two versions, two prototypes for the final script. Had the Torah imparted only one of the two exodus stories, we would, of necessity, had only one possible ending for Jewish history. If, for example, we had the

---

9. Commentary of the Vilna Gaon to the *Tikkunei Zohar Tikkun* 11.

Exodus from Egypt as the sole prototype, the final redemption would, of necessity, have the same ending: The Jews will be saved at the expense of their enemies. This is the incredible insight of the Vilna Gaon: The Exodus from Egypt was itself based on the exodus from the house of Lavan. So many of the details are identical that we can see how that earlier exodus created the energy for the subsequent exodus. Yet the conclusions are starkly different, and herein lies the challenge of history: The existence of that earlier exodus with its own conclusion creates an alternative—an alternative that was available to Pharaoh, as it was available to others who hosted the Jewish People throughout history. So many times, this alternative has been rejected; so many times, Pharaoh and others of his ilk created a zero-sum game, leaving the scenario in which Yaakov and Lavan made peace an unrealized potential. This conclusion, this alternative ending, is still available. This spiritual dynamic is at least as valid, if not more so, than the other, harder route that has been chosen too many times by too many of our enemies.

The Vilna Gaon teaches us that the Torah tells the same story twice; there are two possible endings to the story. We have no trouble identifying with the theme of being pursued by an enemy or a potential adversary who has not treated us with the respect we deserve. The part of the story in which the Jews are saved is familiar to us; as in the past, we will be redeemed. The question is, what happens to the "other"? Must history end with lifeless bodies floating on the sea? While this final scene of vengeance and retribution may appeal to the baser elements of human nature, is this the *denouement* we must necessarily anticipate? Or does the story end with mutual respect, reconciliation and covenant? One story, twice told, with two possible final scenes: Which ending do we really want? Which one do we pray for? Which one do we hope to witness—"speedily and in our own times"?

Parashat Vayishlach
Confronting Your Fears

Yaakov's return to Israel would not be simple; the factors that caused him to flee all those years earlier had not changed. His mother Rivka, who said she would send for him when his brother's murderous anger subsided, had not contacted him. To the best of his knowledge, his brother Esav was lying in wait, plotting deadly revenge. Nonetheless, Yaakov was coming back. What awaited him on the other side of the Jordan River was unknown, unclear; the only certainty was the fear in his heart. The dread and anticipation of catastrophe would have paralyzed a lesser man; sometimes, fear is worse than the catastrophe itself. Yet Yaakov marched on, deliberately but cautiously.

In fact, his fears were not unfounded. He had no illusions about the nature of his adversary: He had begun wrestling with his brother *in utero*, leaving their mother Rivka distressed and bewildered enough to seek Divine guidance. This was no ordinary morning sickness, nor was their struggle the normal movement experienced in a twin pregnancy: God informed her that she was carrying two distinct nations that would be at odds for millennia.

Apart from the personal history between himself and Esav, Yaakov had another reason for concern: As the sun set, Yaakov was alone, and he was accosted by an unknown assailant. This was certainly not a good omen. In fact, rabbinic tradition identifies this nocturnal opponent as the spiritual power of his brother Esav.

In short, the confrontation he was about to face had been twice foreshadowed, first by the struggle in Rivka's womb, and again in the dark of the night before the actual encounter. To make matters worse, as the sun rises, Esav approaches with four hundred ruffians. Yaakov's chances of survival seem dismal.

And then, something strange happens: The ruffians turn out to be no more than a benign prop, part of the scenery; Esav is overcome with emotion and fraternal goodwill. The two brothers forge an understanding. Twenty years of fear, dread and anger melt away in a brotherly bear hug; friendly chatter takes the place of violence.

As readers, this turn of events is more than unexpected; it seems the plot has taken an unimaginable turn. We have been witnessing the drama unfold for several chapters, watching the characters develop, feeling their animosity build. We have been waiting for the unavoidable collision, for the other shoe to drop. The loaded gun, as it were, was introduced in the first act of this family's story, and we fully expect that it will be fired in this climactic scene. Is it possible that Yaakov wrestles with Esav as a fetus, and again with his angel, yet when they finally meet on level ground, as two grown men who are prepared for violent confrontation, they settle their differences peacefully? What went wrong—or should we ask, what went right?

We may posit that the strange confrontation in the night changed the course of Yaakov's confrontation with Esav the following morning: By defeating Esav's spiritual representative, Yaakov had deflated his flesh-and-blood adversary.

Perhaps there is a more powerful lesson to be learned from the surprise outcome of this story: Even when all the signs point in one direction, history is not predetermined. Spiritual imprints may have been made by our personal or family history; precedents may exist in our relationships. Nonetheless, each of us is capable of changing the course of history, of rewriting the script. Our personal and collective fate is not predetermined; outcomes are neither prearranged nor immutable. Cycles can be broken—cycles of violence, cycles of abuse, cycles of enmity. We can determine our future.

Despite premonitions, precedents, signs and omens, Yaakov uses his prayers and the skills he has acquired from a lifetime of living by his wits to extricate himself from what seemed an impossible situation. The message for all of us is that we must not let our past determine our future. We must not allow dreams or signs to dictate how things will work out. We must take control, and truly believe that God has entrusted us with freedom of choice. We may not always succeed, but we must not allow past failures to determine our future. Sometimes, despite all the evidence to the contrary, things do work out. Just ask Yaakov.

Parashat Vayeshev
A Contentious Coat

To some it seems to be a story about a coat, a dazzling coat of many colors, but in truth, it was never about the coat; the coat was merely a symbol. It symbolized love, it symbolized hatred, and it symbolized jealousy. Funny how an inanimate object can generate so much emotion and passion, how it can tear a family apart, and lead to the very brink of murder.

The coat was striking, regal; it made whoever wore it look royal, like a sovereign. Yaakov gave the coat to Yosef because he loved him, but that striped symbol of favoritism meant many things to many people. His brothers hated the coat and its implication of subservience, and they hated Yosef. And even though they may have denied it, they had no respect for their father who gave Yosef the coat and determined that Yosef alone should wear it. Though they may not have seen it that way, the brothers' perfidy was not only toward Yosef, it was also toward their father.

We can imagine that Yosef wore his coat of many colors with pride, strutting about like a peacock. When his brothers ripped it off of him in a fit of murderous rage, they added one more color: stark red, the color of blood.

Yosef survived, humiliated and humbled but alive: What could easily have deteriorated into a murderous lynching was tamed, and murder averted. Yosef was "only" sold off as a slave. His airs of importance were tempered, but only temporarily:

Later, Yosef would once again be dressed in royal garb, and his leadership and superiority would be recognized and celebrated far and wide. Whether or not his brothers were willing to acknowledge it, Yosef looked good in royal clothing.

Of all the brothers, it was Yehuda who suggested that they sell Yosef rather than kill him, despite the fact that, of all the brothers, Yehuda may have had the most to lose from Yosef's preferred status. Reuven, Shimon and Levi, Yaakov's three oldest sons, had each proven unworthy of the leadership role, and the next in line was Yehuda. Yehuda's descendants would establish the unending chain of Jewish monarchy, through the Davidic line. Perhaps Yehuda, more than the other brothers, saw Yosef wearing the clothes of royalty as an historic error: If anyone was to be anointed, dressed in royal garb and set above the others, it should have been he. The coat of many colors should have been his, and Yosef was usurping his rightful place, staging a sort of coup. Yehuda could have been the first to justify putting his younger brother to death. However, in a gesture of benevolence befitting a king, Yehuda suggested that it would be sufficient punishment to sell Yosef as a lowly slave and strip him of the undeserved trappings of royalty, the coat. This was Yehuda's attempt to restore order. Far from feeling that he had perpetrated an act of horrific cruelty on an undeserving younger brother, Yehuda must have felt like a benevolent monarch.

History has a way of evening the score. Centuries later, when Yehuda's descendant David was anointed as King of Israel, the royal clothing finally came to its rightful owner. In one of the Torah's great ironies, the only other biblical characters who wore coats of many colors were King David's children, Yehuda's descendants—most notably, Tamar.[10] But in tragic, haunting irony, the beautiful coat did not bring her any more joy or dignity than it had brought to Yosef.

---

10. 2 Samuel 13:18.

44

At face value, Tamar suffered from a problem that was the opposite of Yosef's: Her brothers did not hate her, they loved her. Her half-brother, Amnon, loved her in a way that a brother should not love a sister; in reality, the love he professed for his half-sister was no more than carnal lust. In a fit of violence, Amnon ripped off Tamar's clothing and raped her. After he had his way with her, Amnon discarded and humiliated her, and came to hate her; to Amnon, Tamar had become a constant reminder of his own weakness. Tamar tore her colorful coat as a sign of mourning, desecrating her royal clothing as a reflection of the desecration she had suffered.

Soon enough, her other brother Avshalom, who loved her in a more normal, fraternal way, exacted vengeance and killed Amnon. In time, Avshalom mounted a full-scale rebellion against his father David; the cycle of jealousy, treason, and betrayal comes to its tragic close only with the death of Avshalom.

The story of Amnon, Tamar, and Avshalom is intricately bound up with the story of Yosef and his brothers. Both stories revolve around a beautiful, favored child, a coat of many colors denoting royalty, and rebellion against the father. The family of the perpetrator in the first story becomes the victim in the second episode. Karma can be cruel: Sometimes the very same crimes we perpetrate against others have a way of coming back to punish us. Such was the story of the coat of many colors, the coat of love, hate, jealousy, rebellion and murder.

Parashat Miketz
Victim No More

Yosef is one of the most impressive characters in the Torah. Although he faced seemingly insurmountable challenges, he remained strong, focused, dedicated, where others would surely have given up.

His mother died when he was young, and when his father filled the gap with twice as much love, his half-siblings responded with hatred and jealousy. Those closest to him conspired to murder him. He was kidnapped; he was sold as a slave. He was wooed by his boss's wife and then framed when he did not capitulate to her lewd advances. He was imprisoned. And yet, despite all of these experiences, he never lost his dignity or his faith.

In fact, God is always in Yosef's thoughts and in his words. He speaks of God to the libidinous Mrs. Potifar. He speaks of God to his fellow inmates. He speaks of God to his brothers, even when they do not recognize him and believe him to be an Egyptian despot. Perhaps most impressively, he speaks of God to Pharaoh, a man who thinks of himself as a deity.

A lesser man than Yosef would have carefully crafted his speech to endear himself to the Egyptian leader. Yosef is given an opportunity to position himself as an advisor to Pharaoh; his freedom, if not his very life, hinges upon this dialogue. Rather than taking credit for his ability to interpret dreams, rather than talking up his own skill and insight, Yosef explains that he does not possess any personal talent; it is God who knows all. Rather than highlighting or aggrandizing his abilities, which are so crucial for Pharaoh, he takes no credit. Instead, Yosef demurs and speaks only of God. This is certainly a dangerous strategy to employ when dealing with Pharaoh—yet it succeeds.

Yosef includes God in his every move and speaks of God's presence in every situation. In a sense, the feeling is reciprocal: God is clearly with him in all he does. Everyone around him (other than his brothers) sees it, from Pharaoh to the lowliest Egyptian. Yosef sees God's hand in every situation, and, through Yosef, the hand of God becomes apparent to others, who recognize that Yosef is blessed and God is the secret of his success. Yosef succeeds in bringing God-consciousness into the lives he touches, but even more striking is that he brings God Himself, as it were, into the bitter exile in Egypt: God is with him in the House of Potifar, God is with him in prison, and God is with him when he enters the palace, a place many others thought only had room for one (imagined) deity.

Yosef even sees that God was with him when he was sold: When his brother's recoil from his presence, Yosef comforts them by sharing his certainty that it was not they but God who brought him to Egypt.

Keeping all of this in mind, we can understand why, in the one instance that Yosef complains and sounds like a victim, the rabbinic commentaries express bitter disappointment.[11]

Yosef explains the dream of the wine steward, and gives him so much more than a mere prediction of his future: It is God, Yosef explains, who controls the world; it is God who has revealed the dream, and it is God who will see to it that he will soon be reinstated to his former position. At the same time, Yosef pleads that he not be forgotten, and begs his fellow inmate to help him leave his prison cell.

---

11. See Rashi, *Bereishit* 40:23.

This must surely have seemed like a mixed message: If God is so intimately involved, why would Yosef turn to a prisoner, or even to Pharaoh's wine steward, for help? When Yosef's name is eventually put forth as a potential dream interpreter, the steward does not mention God or Yosef's unique connection to God's plan. While this may have been due to the wine steward's assessment that mentioning another God in Pharaoh's presence would be impolitic, the truth may be somewhat harder: Asking the steward for help was counter-productive in terms of Yosef's larger mission—to spread monotheism. The steward was left with the impression that the young man he met in prison had a quirky ability to understand dreams; the God of whom Yosef spoke left no impression, having been undercut by Yosef's plea.

For this, the Rabbis claim, Yosef languished in prison an extra two years. His "crime" was not that he attempted to free himself, but that he removed God from the consciousness of those around him. Only when Yosef, in a moment of weakness, describes himself as a victim of human injustice and pleads for the wine steward's help, does he actually become a victim.

For Yosef, this was a one-time lapse, which was immediately rectified when he stood before Pharaoh. Once again, Yosef ascribes all the power and knowledge to God, and there is no hint of the sense of victimization that was discernible in Yosef's speech to the wine steward. When Yosef regains his faith and his vision, when he reminds himself—and Pharaoh, and all of Egypt—that God is in the driver's seat, God's involvement in human history becomes evident to all those around him. Yosef is immediately catapulted to a position of power, the victor rather than the victim.

This is one of Yosef's many lessons to us all: Even in the most difficult situations, when we believe that God has engineered events for our ultimate benefit, we are not victims of fate, but living testament to God's power and ultimate kindness.

Parashat Vayigash
A Moment of Truth

We like to tell lies—little lies. Often we are so convincing that we ourselves believe these lies. They become part of our personal narrative, part of our personal truth. The emotional comfort they bring is addictive, especially when the real historical truth is most difficult. We banish the uncomfortable truth, send it into exile in a distant parallel universe that we ignore, if at all possible. Sometimes these "little" lies are not so little; we build a persona out of lies that we present to the world, but the true identity that lies behind the façade of lies is a pathetic version of the caricature we have created.

Yosef's (half) brothers lived a lie—a pathetic lie, but a beautiful lie. The lie was of a united, loving family. The lie was the love they professed for their father. The lie was the charade of mutual responsibility. Under the veneer of that lie stood a stark truth: The brother whom they laconically described as "no longer (with us)" quite ironically, actually was with them, listening attentively to their every word. He questioned, he probed, he tested them—and he knew they were lying. Their answers were vague and mysterious; they simply said, "He is not with us," implying that this brother was dead, or perhaps that he had chosen to part ways with them, had gone in search of fame and fortune.

What they neglected to mention was the circumstances behind their brother's mysterious disappearance. They failed to mention the ugly truth: Their brother had not simply vanished. Someone had plotted to kill him; someone had attacked him, jumped him, stripped him of his clothing and threw him, scared and trembling, into a cold, dark pit. They failed to mention that they themselves were that "someone." They failed to mention that a group of people sat to have a pleasant lunch within earshot of this brother's bloodcurdling screams coming from the nearby pit; again, they failed to mention that they themselves were the members of this callous group. They failed to mention that someone sold him as a slave; and once again that "someone" was they. They preferred the lie of "he is no longer (with us)." Simple, uncomplicated, far less emotional and messy: In Hebrew, their lie is even more elegant. It took only one word to bury the truth: *einenu (Bereishit 42:13)*.

Yosef listens to the lie, he hears the new narrative and he waits as they proceed to show off their beautiful family and their beautiful family values. They are united. Yosef sets a trap and puts his goblet in the bag of his brother Binyamin. Will the others rally around even *this* brother, the second son of Rachel, Yosef's full brother? Or will they abandon him as they had abandoned Yosef all those years ago? Will they turn their backs on Binyamin when he cries out to them, when he is frightened and vulnerable?

Yehuda responds with righteous indignation. He pleads, he cajoles and he lectures the man he believes to be an unyielding Egyptian despot. And then he moves to guilt. He explains that separating their father from the son he loves would be cruel, possibly even fatal for their elderly father. In this new narrative, Yosef would be made to bear the guilt for breaking up this beautiful family. Yosef would be the one to break their father's heart, and possibly to kill the old man with grief.

At that moment Yosef reveals his true self. He speaks one short sentence, and deals the brothers an impossible dose of truth. The man facing them is Yosef, the victim of their heinous acts. The narrative they have been selling him is fiction; he knows it and they know it. Their carefully constructed lie implodes; their narrative crashes and burns when their victim stands before them as their tormentor.

The rabbis use this moment of stark truth as an analogy for the moment that awaits each of us when our days on this earth are done. At the end of our lives, each of us will stand in front of God with our own carefully crafted narrative, only to have the inescapable truth contradict our lies. The further from the truth we have spun our narrative, the greater will be the shattering force of confronting the truth. If we are to withstand that confrontation, we best prepare for it by examining the truth of our lives, and guiding our narrative in anticipation of that great and awesome moment. Otherwise, we will stand stunned and paralyzed, just as Yosef's brothers stood before him—shocked into silence.[12]

At the very moment he forces the brothers to face the truth and grapple with the full force of their actions, Yosef does the impossible: He slips into their narrative of unity and love. Yosef prefers their fiction over his own truth, a truth filled with so many physical and emotional scars. And when Yosef embraces their narrative of love, he turns the fiction into fact. Only through Yosef can this family's scars be healed. Only when Yosef comes back into their lives can they become the united family that existed in their fantasy narrative; only now can the lies be replaced with love.

---

12. Talmud Bavli *Chagigah* 4b.

Parashat Vay'chi
An Inconclusive Conclusion

As the book of *Bereishit* nears its conclusion, there is some "unfinished" business to be tended to. At first glance the issue is a local one, concerning a topic that has been hovering over the past few chapters: The reconciliation between Yosef and his brothers. While our initial impression is that in *Parashat Vayigash*, the brothers had buried the hatchet in dramatic fashion, there was something unsettling, something one-sided about their rapprochement.

We hear Yosef's words, and feel the raw emotion as he reveals to the sons of Yaakov that the man who has been tormenting them is none other than their long-lost brother. But what of the brothers? The Torah does not tell us what they said or, perhaps more importantly, what they felt. Did they finally come to see him as their brother? Did they see the error of their ways? Did they apologize to him? And even if they could not wrap their mouths around those difficult words, if they did not come to love or respect him, did they accept Yosef's dreams not as delusional or self-serving, but as an accurate prediction of the future? Any intelligent observer, any reader of the text sensitive to the symbolic messages of Yosef's dreams, is forced to acknowledge that Yosef's dreams of economic and political superiority were clearly fulfilled. Did the brothers finally grasp the full import of Yosef's dreams, and accept the fact that Yosef had vision that far surpassed their own?

A River Flowed from Eden

Parashat Vay'chi records the passing of Yaakov. Tragically, upon Yaakov's death, the brothers plead with Yosef not to exact revenge upon them. They tell Yosef that on his deathbed, their father had ordered Yosef to do them no harm. They beg him to spare their lives and let them live out their days as his slaves.[13] Although the Talmud debates[14] whether or not Yaakov had actually addressed his sons' relationships with one another on his deathbed, or whether the brothers had concocted this dying wish for self-preservation, the painful truth is the same: Apparently, after all these years, the brothers still do not trust Yosef. Perhaps they suspect that his words of reconciliation had been motivated by political expedience: In his glorified position it was unseemly that he had no family, no past. Perhaps they suspected that he tolerated their presence only as a means of reuniting with his beloved father. The Torah records Yosef's impassioned speech on this occasion as well: Once again, after 17 years as their protector and benefactor, Yosef assures his brothers of his fidelity toward them. But did they believe him? Was the relationship healed?

Parashat Vay'chi is the final chapter of the book of *Bereishit*, in which the end of the story of a family is the beginning of the story of a nation. And yet, there is this uncertainty, this lack of resolution. Is this really the proper way to end a book, or to begin the epic tale of the origins of the Nation of Israel?

Perhaps a look back at the beginning of the book will help us appreciate its conclusion: The first two brothers, Cain and Abel, were murderer and victim respectively. Fraternal jealousy led to fratricide. As the chapters unfold, we find so many brothers who do not get along that we are quickly convinced this is in fact one of the major themes if the book: *Bereishit* may be seen, not unjustifiably, as the story of sibling rivalry and family discord.

---

13. *Bereishit* 50:15-21.
14. Talmud Bavli *Yevamot* 65b.

And that may be the greatness of the book's conclusion: Despite the jealousy and hatred the brothers had for Yosef, they do not resort to bloodshed. As is sometimes the case, the moral choice is no more than the lesser of two evils. The sale of Yosef is preferable to the murder of Abel at the hands of Cain, or to the fate Yaakov would have suffered by Esav's hand had God not intervened. Although the progress may seem small, it is progress nonetheless.

But the book does not end with the sale of Yosef. It does not end with Yosef overcoming impossible odds and rising to greatness. It ends as Yosef forgives his brothers, and cares for them for the rest of his life. This is true greatness of spirit. From beginning to end, the brothers' attitude toward Yosef ranges from outright animosity to ambivalence, yet they overcome their impulse to kill him, and Yosef takes their entire history to a new level when he forgives them. Framed in these terms, as we compare the morality exhibited in the beginning of the book to the end, mankind's progress becomes apparent; even in this sordid tale, some light shines through. The first steps to nationhood are taken when we finally become a family.

ספר
שמות

Parashat Shemot
A New Book, An Old Story

This *parashah* is the first in a new book. It represents a new beginning, not only of the narrative, but of the nation whose narrative it contains. And yet, so many of the elements of *Shemot*—both the *parashah* and the entire book which bears its name—seem strangely familiar, yet different to their parallels in the book of *Bereishit*. Are these elements of importance, or are they merely generic, stock "props" of epic literature? In other words, are there narrative elements in common between *Bereishit* and *Shemot*, or is our overactive imagination deluding us? And if these elements are, in fact, revisited, what is their significance? How is this new book connected to the previous book? To what extent is this a new beginning, and to what extent is *Shemot* a thematic continuation of *Bereishit*?

Let us consider some of the smaller details that may or may not connect the two books: *Shemot* finds the nascent nation on the banks of the Nile, a life-giving river that is reminiscent of the rivers that flowed from Eden and watered the land. In each of the books, we are introduced to one special tree—a tree that is unique, a tree that somehow enlightens. Although the burning bush is not off limits, Moshe immediately understands that it is to be observed from a respectful distance, and not to be approached. Similarly, when his staff is transformed into a serpent, Moshe recoils; perhaps he is reminded of an old adversary. We have seen the serpent before and the results were devastating.

The larger picture bears far more resemblance than the details that comprise it. In a sense, the entire Exodus story has already been told in microcosm in *Bereishit*, and the book of *Shemot* may be seen as an expansion, a retelling on a national scale, of the same story: famine had driven Avraham and Sarah to Egypt. After arriving there, Avraham sensed that his life, as a male, was in danger, while Sarah was the object of the Egyptians' desire. As a result of Pharaoh's treatment of Avraham and Sarah, the palace was struck with plagues; Avraham and his family left with great wealth, and Hagar, quite possibly the princess of Egypt, throws in her lot with Avraham and Sarah, and returns with them to become a part of their household in the Land of Canaan.[15]

So, too, with the descendants of Avraham and Sarah generations later: To escape famine in the Land of Israel, the sons of Israel went to Egypt, where they flourished. The Egyptian king plotted to dispose of the males and co-opt the females. God then struck the Egyptians with fearsome plagues, and the Children of Israel left Egypt with their heads held high, greatly enriched by the ordeal. The Egyptian princess who had saved Moshe and raised him in the palace, joined the Israelites on their grand march to freedom and independence.[16]

Other episodes from *Bereishit* have echoes in the book of *Shemot* as well: In *Bereishit*, the terrible flood eradicated almost all of mankind; in *Shemot*, the Jewish People was threatened with annihilation by the decree to cast all the male children into the raging waters of the Nile. In *Bereishit*, one righteous man was singled out, and he and his family were saved by the ark in which they weathered the storm that destroyed the rest of the world. In *Shemot*, one righteous child is saved in an ark, but he becomes the catalyst for the salvation not only of his

15. See Ramban, *Bereishit* 12:10.
16. See 1 *Divrei Ha-Yamim* 4:18.

own family, but for the entire House of Israel. As is so often the case in *Shemot*, the particular becomes magnified. Personal narratives from the book of *Bereishit* are the buds from which the larger narrative of a nation will blossom.

Shemot, then, is a new book that revisits and develops old themes, shifting from micro to macro concerns. And yet, the resolutions in the Book of *Shemot* are far more hopeful: Whereas *Bereishit* recounted cataclysmic destruction of civilization—total destruction and rebirth after the "purifying" waters of the flood, the annihilation of the generation of the Tower of Babel, the eradication of Sodom and Amorah—*Shemot* is essentially a tale of redemption. The lad in the ark will not merely save himself; he will see to it that all of the Children of Israel make it through the sea. Time and again, Moshe will avert the annihilation of the sinners and reject God's offer to start a new nation through him, much like He did with Noach. In the Book of *Shemot*, the redemption of one leads to the redemption of many; the emergence of Moshe and the emergence of the Nation of Israel hold within them the key to the redemption of all of humanity.

Parashat Va'Era
Pharaoh's Conundrum

As the showdown between God and Pharaoh nears its apex, we are faced with a moral dilemma that has far-reaching ramifications. It may be argued that Pharaoh is no more than a pawn in a cosmic drama, since the enslavement of the Jews was pre-determined, and had been foretold to Avraham hundreds of years earlier.[17] To what extent, then, did Pharaoh have free will? To what extent did he deserve the severe punishment meted out to him? Any competent defense attorney engaged to defend Pharaoh might choose between several different strategies. On the one hand, the defense could point out, Pharaoh was simply carrying out the will of God; if anything, he deserved kudos, not Divine wrath. Alternatively, Pharaoh could claim a lack of culpability due to diminished capacity: God Himself had "hardened" his heart. Was he at liberty to have behaved any other way?

A close reading of the biblical text disqualifies both of these defense strategies: As far as diminished capacity is concerned, the text clearly indicates that Pharaoh's heart was manipulated by God only after Pharaoh himself had displayed arrogance and a stubborn streak. Through the first five plagues, Pharaoh hardened his own heart. He needed no coercing to issue decrees that made the Israelites' lives unbearable, nor did he come

---

17. *Bereishit* 15:13-14.

under any undue influence when he refused to heed Moshe's calls before, during and after the plagues of blood, frogs, lice, wild beasts and pestilence. In fact, one could argue that by subsequently "hardening" his heart, God allowed Pharaoh to continue to travel down the path he had already chosen. Pharaoh had clearly indicated his attitude toward the Children of Israel; the plagues were events of such tremendous supernatural interference in the course of history that they effectively denied him the ability to continue to conduct the affairs of state in the manner he had chosen. By hardening his heart, God allowed Pharaoh to continue to make his own choices in the face of crushing supernatural force. God's intervention, then, gave Pharaoh back his free will, as opposed to taking it away.

As for the contention that Pharaoh should have been rewarded because he was "on a mission from God," rather than punished for his treatment of the Israelites, Pharaoh's own words belie this claim: What sort of messenger of God, upon being confronted by Moshe, denies any knowledge of God and refuses to accept the word of His prophet? Moreover, the predetermined slavery that had been foretold to Avraham did not specify where the slavery would take place or what its nature would be. Pharaoh could easily have abdicated the role of enslaver, refused to assume the morally reprehensible position of oppressor. Furthermore, the covenant that God forged with Avraham spoke of enslavement and suffering, but did not speak of infanticide. The sheer cruelty displayed by Pharaoh went far beyond the call of duty.

From the outset, Pharaoh expressed an objective problem with the Israelites. He regarded them as a fifth column, strangers, foreigners residing in "his" land, a people who could not be trusted. Ironically, the Israelites had been in the land of

Egypt for generations, and the Egyptian economy had been saved by none other than an Israelite. Yet Pharaoh chose not to study history; he did not remember Yosef.

Pharaoh could have chosen another way to solve the problem he perceived: Rather than victimizing or ostracizing these strangers, he could have co-opted them, subsumed them into the greater Egyptian nation (a nation that had successfully subsumed waves of foreigners from the north). By affording them full rights, acceptance, appreciation, he could have turned his "adversaries" into allies. Throughout history, the Children of Israel have always been susceptible to the seductive advances of alien cultures; the astounding rate of assimilation in the modern era speaks eloquently in favor of this strategy. By displaying his distrust of these strangers, by legislating their "otherness," Pharaoh effectively ensured their continued existence as a separate nation, while at the same time sealing his own fate and the fate of his kingdom. Pharaoh had shown his hand: It was not the Will of God that he wished to fulfill, it was his own paranoia and xenophobia that led him down the path he chose.

The Torah's message regarding Pharaoh's choice rings out loud and clear throughout the remainder of the Five Books: We are enjoined, time and time again, to learn from Pharaoh's bad choices. We are commanded to treat the stranger with respect, love and acceptance. We are instilled with an acute sense of history, and taught to distill from the slavery experience what it is like to be disenfranchised. The Torah instructs us to redouble our efforts to see to it that others will not be treated as we were. Like Pharaoh, we are capable of choosing the path of hatred and suspicion or of peace and respect; one of the quintessential principles of Judaism is the moral imperative to choose the path of peace.

Pharaoh made the wrong choice, and neither a good cardiologist nor a sharp defense attorney could have changed the outcome. The choices he made were made freely, willingly, enthusiastically. His misdeeds were his own; his treatment of the emerging Jewish nation was criminal, and his punishment well-deserved.

Parashat Bo
The Dignity of Mitzvot

The time for redemption had arrived. The Jews would be leaving Egypt at last—whether because the pre-ordained period of enslavement had come to an end, or because their situation had become so intolerable that God felt they could not remain in exile any longer. For one reason or the other, God decreed that the time had come to fulfill His covenant with Avraham. The time for the Exodus had arrived.

At this critical juncture, before the Children of Israel begin the next chapter in their history, something transpires that seems, to modern eyes, commonplace or self-evident, yet at this point in history is quite rare: God gives the Israelites commandments, *mitzvot*. In time, *mitzvot* will become a major aspect of the relationship between God and man, but until this point in history, God had not dictated specific behaviors to mankind, with only a few very notable exceptions. The commandments, as a corpus of law, would be given at Mount Sinai months later, forging a new relationship between the Jewish People and God based on a covenant of observance. Why, then, does God deem it necessary to issue commandments prior to the Exodus, prior to the Revelation at Sinai? Why the urgency to take time and attention away from the busy events of the plagues and give Moshe and Aharon commandments to share with the people, commandments to be performed on the very eve of the Exodus?

The Passover Haggadah quotes a verse from the Book of *Yechezkel* (Ezekiel 16:7) in which the Jewish People at the time of the Exodus is compared to a young woman who is "fully developed" but completely naked. The meaning of this image is often lost on readers from societies that are either puritanical or over-sexed—or, like modern Western society, both. This verse is not about sex or the female body *per se*; it is an expression of self-conscious humiliation. The verse describes a young woman who has come of age and begins to experience the self-awareness of her own body, only to find herself exposed, publicly humiliated by her own nakedness.

What is the Haggadah trying to teach us? At the point of the Exodus, the Jews were coming of age as a nation, but at the same time they became acutely aware of their spiritual nakedness. They felt unworthy of redemption. They maintained the collective memory of the covenant with Avraham and the promise of their great destiny, but at the same time they felt that they were undeserving beneficiaries of God's contractual obligation to their ancestors.

In Egypt, the Jews had failed to live up to Avraham's legacy. They had not effectively spread monotheism. In fact, rabbinic tradition tells us that they had neglected the covenant between God and Avraham by failing to circumcise their sons. Even worse, as they morphed from an extended family into a distinct nation, the niche they had carved out was not based upon their singular beliefs or practices, nor upon their unique moral stance in the face of the corruption of Egypt, but rather as a people who could not be trusted, the quintessential outsiders who survived by exploiting the host society. How had they earned this distasteful reputation? Was it their business practices, or did the Egyptians cultivate the Israelites' "otherness" for their own purposes, resorting to the same accusations that have been wielded against the Jews throughout history as justification to exploit and abuse them?

Whatever the reasons for their sense of humiliation, the imagery used by the Haggadah communicates an almost crippling sense of vulnerability and self-loathing. And at that very moment of crushing self-awareness, God steps in and performs an act of kindness: He gives the Israelites commandments. He engages them, makes a gesture that will allow them to express their desire for spirituality and for self-actualization. He gives them the means to regain their dignity, and to make them feel worthy of redemption. The commandments are to serve as a proverbial cloak with which God helps them cover their nakedness. By giving them commandments, God performs an act of love and respect, and allows them to respond in kind.

The purpose of *mitzvot*—all the commandments, and not only those given to the nation of slaves struggling to find their identity—is to give man dignity, to give us an active role in defining our personal and communal identity and destiny, to give purpose and worth to our lives and to help us feel worthy of our relationship with God. The commandments do the impossible: They allow limited, finite man to have a relationship with an infinite God.

God's gesture of kindness and compassion lies at the heart of our relationship with Him, as well as our interpersonal relationships: The underlying principle of our treatment of others is the compassion we learn from God Himself. This tenet of our faith may be most clearly discerned in the laws of charity (*tzedakah*). We are taught that the highest level of *tzedakah* is to give a person in need a job.[18] The real gift of *tzedakah* is not dollars and cents; it is the restoration of self-worth, the rehabilitation of our fellow man to a place of dignity. This, we are taught, is true *hesed*; this is how we emulate God.

---

18. Rambam, "Laws of Gifts to the Poor" 10:7.

As the Children of Israel stood on the cusp of redemption, they lacked the critical elements of freedom: self-awareness and dignity. To be truly free, they had to move past the feeling that they were unworthy of redemption. To return to Yechezkel's metaphor, God offered this maiden, now fully-grown, beautiful, regal clothing; in an act of love and respect, God extended lavish adornments to help her overcome her humiliating nakedness, and at the same time expressed their special intimacy. He helped her see herself as worthy of His love, before carrying her off into the desert to begin their new life together. In a gesture of kindness and generosity, God gave us *mitzvot* to clothe us and adorn us, to make us feel special, beautiful—and worthy of His love. This is why some commentators see the root of the word *mitzvah* not in the word *tzivvui,* "command," but in *tzavta,* "togetherness."[19] This is the sentiment expressed in the subsequent verses of Yechezkel's metaphor: After describing the maiden's humiliation, the verses continue, "I came to you and saw you, and behold, it was your time, the time for love. I spread the hem of my cloak over you and covered your nakedness; I made a promise to you and entered into a covenant with you, [by the] word of the Almighty God—and you became Mine."

---

19. See *Sefer Shnei Luchot ha-Brit, Yoma; Derech Chaim, Tochechat Musar* section 16.

Parashat B'Shalach
The Long Shortcut

When the Israelites finally leave Egypt, rather than taking them on the shortest, most direct route to their destination, God leads them on a circuitous path. The trip eventually becomes so long that almost an entire generation passes away and the overwhelming majority of the adults who leave Egypt never make it to the Promised Land. One might be tempted to regard this entire venture as a failure. However, at the very start of the journey, the Torah tells us that God took them on this longer route because they did not have the moral fortitude to take the shorter route.

Perhaps it is human nature that makes detours infuriating; any trip that takes longer than scheduled can make us bristle. Maybe we are hardwired to want to shorten our travels, and arrive at our destination in as short a time as possible. For most of us, the only thing better than arriving on time is finding a shortcut and arriving early, especially when we are going home.

But travel is not always about geography, about movement from one place to another; travel is not only result-oriented. Sometimes the places, experiences and people we meet along the way are really the point of the trip. Sometimes the journey is not about the destination, but rather the growth experienced along the way.

The Israelites had been thrust into freedom, but the generations of slavery had limited and stifled them in so many ways, "relieving" them of the burden of independent thought and initiative. Incongruously, slaves and prisoners often create a "comfort zone" of rote functionality. Their lack of freedom can become like a womb or a cocoon, limiting yet sustaining. Without exercise, innate creativity and even the instinct for self-preservation become dull. People who become accustomed to having their basic needs taken care of by their captors or masters quickly lose the ability to take responsibility for their own lives. This is not a mass occurrence of Stockholm syndrome, in which the slaves identify with their oppressors. The dynamic is far more subtle: Slaves quickly "learn their place" and begin to believe that this is their fate. The security of the present—even an oppressive present—often outweighs the frightening prospect of the unknown, of the uncharted road to freedom and independence.

Had the Israelites taken the direct route to the Promised Land, they would have faced war, on the one hand, and economic independence on the other. Physically, emotionally, and spiritually, they were not prepared for either, as is evidenced by their recurring bouts of nostalgia for the "good old days in Egypt." Their long, circuitous journey through the desert, then, was an educational and spiritual process of growth. In the course of their travels, they would reexamine their dependency. Their most basic needs would become acute, pressing, in a new and alarming way, and they would learn to turn to God, and not to Pharaoh, as the ultimate Provider and Sustainer.

God knew that these newly freed slaves were not yet capable of providing for themselves. Their spiritual and physical capabilities required nurturing. In the desert, they would develop a unique and intimate relationship with God, while at the same time evolving from a rag-tag band of emancipated slaves to a nation capable of defending itself and its right to exist and control its own destiny. For this to happen, the journey would have to be long and the pace slow but deliberate. They would be given commandments, but they would slowly assume responsibility for fulfilling those commandments over time. At the point of the Exodus, they were physically and emotionally exhausted; they had been enslaved and abused for hundreds of years. Had God not intervened, Pharaoh would not have granted them even the three-day vacation Moshe had requested on their behalf. They were in no state to carry all of the burdens of independence. Thus, while they would be granted the Sabbath—a revolutionary concept for the slave mentality—God knew they were not really ready for the six-day working week. They would have to learn about the true source of their sustenance without the physical labor of agrarian life in their homeland.

For that generation, then, the message of Shabbat was learned when on the seventh day they did not collect the manna that fell from heaven throughout the week. Their "work" would be minimal, but the thrust of the lesson—that sustenance comes from God and not Pharaoh—would be clear and unmistakable nonetheless. The spiritual reality they experienced in the desert would achieve an even higher level on Shabbat by the simple cessation of activity, in imitation of God.

This was one of the many lessons they learned on the road, a lesson independent of their ultimate destination; the journey itself would teach them so many more invaluable lessons. The longer, less direct route would allow them to grow in so many ways, while the shorter route would have brought them to their destination long before they were ready to meet the challenges that awaited them there, long before they would truly be worthy of the inheritance that awaited them at the journey's end. Perhaps the same holds true for our personal journeys in life: The path we take, and the lessons we learn along the way, are often no less important than the destination.

Parashat Yitro
The Good, the Bad, and the Indifferent

After the Israelites escape the Egyptians and survive the skirmish with Amalek, word of their adventures reaches Yitro (Jethro), Moshe's father-in-law. Yitro travels to see his son-in-law and join the Jews' celebration. As it is described in the text, their reunion is touching and emotional, not only on a personal level but also because Yitro expresses wonderment and gratitude for the great miracles God has performed in redeeming, protecting and sustaining the Jewish People. Yitro's feelings of happiness and empathy seem sincere and earnest.

Rabbinic tradition provides us with certain biographical details about Yitro that serve as a fascinating backdrop to this warm reunion. According to this tradition, some years before, Yitro had served as an advisor to Pharaoh, one of a panel of three respected consultants assembled to address Egypt's "Jewish Problem"; the other members of the panel were Bil'am and Iyov (Job). For reasons real or imagined, Pharaoh had begun to identify the Jews as a "fifth column," a foreign element harboring dual loyalties at the very least, or at worst a seditious sub-culture that posed a clear and imminent threat to the stability of Egypt. Three of the world's most respected thinkers were gathered to draft a policy and chart Egypt's response.[20]

Each of the three members of this advisory panel suggested a different course of action. Bil'am, ever the misanthrope,

---

20. Talmud Bavli *Sotah* 11a.

advised that Pharaoh implement a "final solution" to rid Egypt (and the world) of these dangerous aliens. Yitro, on the other hand, spoke out in defense of the Jews, and appealed to Pharaoh on their behalf, advising Pharaoh to adopt a course of peaceful co-existence and understanding. The third advisor, Iyov, was silent. He voiced no opinion, choosing neutrality in a conflict he felt was none of his concern and in which he had no interest.

Pharaoh chose the course plotted by Bil'am, and the final solution was set in motion: All male Jewish infants would be killed at birth, and the females would be subsumed into Egypt's patrilineal society. The Jewish People would cease to exist when its utility as a slave-labor force was outlived. Having fulfilled its mandate, the committee was disbanded, and the advisors went their separate ways. Bil'am collected his reward and made his way home to a hero's welcome, biding his time and grooming his reputation until such time as he would be called upon once again to offer his services as an enemy of the Jewish People. Yitro, whose humanism had turned him into a *persona non grata* in Egypt's poisoned climate of paranoia and hatred, fled to Midian. Iyov, still silent, headed home to the Land of Utz (Oz).

The information we are given about Yitro shines a new light on his joyful reunion with the Israelites in the desert. His happiness is much more than the relieved response of a father-in-law whose son-in-law has narrowly escaped from peril. Yitro has always believed in co-existence, and his path has been vindicated. However, the background provided by this rabbinic teaching goes far beyond Yitro as an individual. On many levels, this tradition offers us a prototype for Jewish foreign policy, as it were: Coming in the wake of the nightmarish experiences of enslavement, abuse and infanticide in Egypt, the certainty of confrontation with the surrounding Philistine culture, and the belligerence and unprovoked violence of the Amalekites, the nascent Jewish nation might have been tempted to adopt a siege mentality regarding all the other nations of the world. Yitro's story illustrated that, their recent experiences notwithstanding, they should not despair of finding individuals and nations that shared the values of humanism and peaceful co-existence.

My teacher, Rabbi Yosef Dov Soloveitchik, suggested that this rabbinic teaching goes far beyond this isolated case, beyond the personal story of Yitro and his relationship with the Jewish People, even beyond the lessons we may learn from his behavior. Rather, it is a timeless observation that imparts profound insight into Jewish thought: Our sages did not believe that non-Jews are by definition good or bad; rabbinic thinking is far more nuanced and far less xenophobic. The story of Pharaoh's advisors is meant to teach us that people, nations, and cultures are not monolithic; some are characterized by empathy while others are defined by hatred. "Advisors" of the type employed by Pharaoh pop up throughout human history; some extend a hand in peace, are open to true dialogue, and offer words of encouragement and sound advice, while others expend their energies plotting ways to make the world *judenrein*. The message of this ancient rabbinic tradition, then, is that we must not lose faith in the possibility of common ground with other cultures and nations. But what of the third group? What are we to make of Iyov, and those whom he represents—those who remain silent? Iyov was neutral; for one reason or another, he declined to takes sides in the conflict between Pharaoh and the Jews. Iyov's stance presents us with an unavoidable moral challenge: Is neutrality in the face of genocide a morally defensible position?[21]

Iyov is certainly not an anonymous character. An entire book of the Bible is devoted to the story of his life, and he is, for all time, a symbol of silence and of suffering. Much like his role

---

21. See *Kol Dodi Dofek: Fate and Destiny* (Ktav), pp. 11ff.

as an advisor to Pharaoh, Iyov is described as a man who did no evil—and therein lies the rub: Iyov was considered, by himself and others, to be a great man precisely because he did no evil. But is this enough? Can moral greatness be equated with the mere avoidance of evil, or does silence in the face of evil make one a silent partner in the atrocity?

Rabbi Soloveitchik suggested that we reconsider Iyov's difficult life story in light of his neutrality: He had managed to ignore the plight of others, to stand by mutely as Jewish children were murdered and an entire nation was vilified, abused and enslaved. The pain and suffering Iyov eventually endures seem to be poetic justice: Iyov is treated to the only pain he can feel—his own.

Iyov, and those who read of his personal suffering, may be tempted to question God's justice and righteousness, but knowing what we now know about his moral stance in Egypt, is it any wonder that God questions Iyov's righteousness? Should it surprise us when Iyov is given a harsh lesson in empathy? Iyov's behavior in Egypt should resonate throughout our reading of the story of his life, and should inform the lesson with which his story concludes: The Book of Iyov comes to an end when he steps outside his own small world and prays for others, finally abandoning his stance of neutrality and insularity. The lesson for our own lives is clear: Only when we learn to care for others can our lives have meaning. Only those who make it their business to feel the pain of others can know true happiness.

Parashat Mishpatim
Minutia

> mi•nu•ti•ae
> mə ˈn(y)o͞oshē ˌē,-shē ˌī/plural noun: minutia
> 1. the small, precise, or trivial details of something: "the minutiae of everyday life"

Some words are upbeat; they energize and inspire us. Other words deflate and confound us. "Spiritual" and "ethereal" are among the former; "minutiae" is a prime example of the latter.

The theophany at Sinai, the spiritual symphony of sight and sound in which God revealed Himself to the Jewish People, embodied all of the uplifting resonance that words are capable of imparting. On the other hand, *Parashat Mishpatim*, with its myriad details and legal minutia, seems more than an anticlimax; we can almost feel the words themselves drag us down from the spiritual heights experienced at Sinai.

Many of us do not love details, especially when we are told what we should do, what we must do, and precisely how we must do it. Our generation is characterized by freelancing, going with the flow, doing "what feels right." Ours is the age in which personal autonomy is regarded as foremost among man's inalienable rights. We find being told what to do stifling and demoralizing. How, then, do we contend with the Torah's shift between the spectacular Revelation of *Parashat Yitro*, when ten magnificent utterances were shared by God that would uplift us by revealing the basis for a lofty existence, and this *parashah*— which goes into painstaking, even painful legal detail?

If we are careful in reading *Parashat Mishpatim*, the transition between these two seemingly different sections appears less a sharp turn and more of a segue: The details contained in this *parashah* are, in fact, intrinsic to the content of the Revelation recounted in the preceding *parashah*. This insight forces us to reconsider the Ten Commandments in a new light: *Parashat Mishpatim* contains a "fleshing out" of the Ten Commandments transmitted at Sinai, which are ten broad principles or categories of law and not particular, specific points.

However, there is a much deeper significance to the juxtaposition of these two different views of Jewish Law. Our understanding should look deeper than the structure of the Torah text, beyond the question of the organization of the material and ideas. The primary issue, the most important question, is the aim of the Revelation itself, and the purpose of the minutiae transmitted immediately in its aftermath. The Revelation at Sinai, the Ten Commandments, and the particulars of law transmitted in *Parashat Mishpatim*, all speak to one central issue: Creating and maintaining a relationship with God.

Man may see himself as a lowly slave, separated from his master by an impossible gulf. We are small and finite, and our Creator is infinite, unapproachable, beyond our understanding. How can the gulf be bridged? How can we come closer to God, involve Him in our lives and elevate ourselves to the point that we are worthy of His love? God gives us responsibilities, drawing us into a proactive, reciprocal relationship. He gives us tasks and taboos that empower us and enable us to give expression to our desire to bridge the chasm that separates us from Him.

For some people, the opportunity to be even a slave to the Almighty is sufficient; the relationship itself is reward enough. For others, the detailed commandments may be framed as terms of endearment: As in the case of loving spouses, intimacy is often expressed by small gestures and behaviors. Gala celebrations and expensive gifts are nice, and are certainly an apt expression of appreciation and emotion, but the big gestures are not the woof and warp of the relationship. The fabric of a loving marriage is woven from details, from everyday kindness, care and consideration. In a loving relationship, these details are neither bothersome, cumbersome nor daunting; rather, they are opportunities to build and grow a relationship, to express appreciation, respect and value. These details are not "minutiae" or annoying demands. They are opportunities— small but constant expressions of love.

When a spouse feels "used" or put upon, enslaved by the gestures or stifled by the restrictions involved in maintaining this relationship, resentful of the small acts of kindness and expressions of love, the relationship becomes dysfunctional. And herein lies the key to understanding *Parashat Mishpatim*, and all of Jewish Law: The ultimate goal is to build a *relationship* with God, with each detailed commandment or restriction representing an opportunity to express our love and appreciation for the myriad gifts and kindnesses, large and small, which God bestows upon us every day. As in interpersonal relationships, true expressions of love that build a relationship—small gifts of flowers or chocolate, a cup of coffee, a smile, any small but meaningful gesture—are to be cherished. They are not "minutiae"; they are, individually and in total, overwhelming expressions of love.

When framed in this manner, legal minutiae are magically transformed into acts and expressions of love, reciprocal gestures that help us build a relationship with God—a relationship that is spiritual and ethereal, uplifting and inspiring.

Parashat Terumah
If You Build It, I Will Come

In five words (which require considerably more to render into understandable English) the Torah commands us to create holiness: "They shall make (for) Me a sanctuary, and I will dwell among them" (*Shemot* 25:8).

What is this commandment? Is God without a home? Does He require shelter? Is He incapable of establishing His presence without a physical structure? Are we building a homestead for God? The second phrase of this commandment clearly states that the result of this building project is not that God will dwell in the new construct, but rather that God will dwell among or within *us*: "and I will dwell within (or among) *them*." God will not be changed by this building; He will not move, as it were, from homelessness to tenancy due to our largesse. The inescapable conclusion, then, is quite the opposite: The human experience has been lacking up to this point. In a spiritual sense, it is man who has been homeless; it is we who need to find our way back home. The commandment to build a sanctuary is an invitation to set aside a place in which we can tap into holiness.

The word *mikdash* (translated as "sanctuary") has at its root the word *kadosh* (holy). What is holiness? What is its source? In biblical Hebrew, *kadosh* (holy) means separate, out of the ordinary, different—even unique. The source of holiness is God, who is unique in every way—separate from the constraints of time, space and matter that rule human experience. In our quest to emulate God, to transcend the limitations of the human condition, we are given the opportunity to create islands of holiness, of unique separation and otherness, in all three dimensions: Shabbat and holidays are islands of holiness in time. Laws that regulate such physical spheres as *kashrut* and ritual purity create islands of holiness in the material world. The commandment to create a sanctuary, a physical place of holiness, allows us to redefine our relationship to space.

When Moshe first saw the burning bush that was not consumed, he came to understand it as a symbol of transcendence. He understood that the God who spoke to him from the burning bush was beyond time, and unconstrained by the laws of physics. What he did not immediately understand was that God had invited him into a holy place, invited him to partake of the holiness. For the first time in human history, God set aside a physical space of holiness, but this was not something Moshe understood intuitively. Therefore, God had to invite Moshe in. God had to explain that man need not recoil from the place of holiness. Moshe was taught to understand the holiness of space, to acknowledge and respect it, but also to stand within it and to take part in it.

This unique place of holiness was marked for all time by the *sneh* (bush) that burned but was not consumed. Moshe had been tending the flocks in what was known as "the mountain of God, at Horev"; after God spoke to him from the burning bush and created this island of holiness, this place became known for all time as Sinai—a word etymologically related to the bush (*sneh*). On that very spot, human history was changed forever: The word of God burst forth. The revelation Moshe experienced at that spot—of the ability to communicate with a God who transcends time, space, and matter—would be repeated, for all of the Jewish People, on that same spot.

The *sneh* (bush) becomes Sinai,[22] and the content of the Revelation that occurred at that place is preserved on the Tablets of Stone, which are then placed in the Ark at the heart of the Sanctuary. The holiness of the place called Sinai is replicated in the creation of the Sanctuary, a unique place that is governed by its own laws of time, space and matter. Eventually, this same holiness will be transferred to the permanent Sanctuary, the Beit HaMikdash—literally, the house of holiness, the Temple in Jerusalem. At the very epicenter of holiness, the Ark that houses the Tablets given at Sinai is protected by two angelic cherubs.

And now we have come full circle. The cherubs that spread their wings over the Ark were last seen in the Garden of Eden, protecting the path to the Tree of Life that stood at the very heart of the Garden. When the world was created, holiness was everywhere—holiness of space, holiness of time and holiness of matter. Yet mankind turned away from holiness and instead chose sin. Exile from the Garden was exile from the holiness of space, from the proximity to God that had been possible in that holy place. At Sinai, that holiness was revealed once again. The building of the Sanctuary, and later the Beit HaMikdash, would give us the opportunity to reestablish that proximity, reconnect with that holiness and bring it into our lives. Building the Sanctuary allows us to end our exile from holiness at last.

The challenge is to take that holiness and bring it into our lives. From time immemorial, man has built great edifices; in fact, it may be said that we have an edifice complex. When we build great structures, we hope to attain a bit of immortality. Of course, we know that immortality eludes us, and all great constructs of stone and mortar will eventually crumble. The only way we can rise above the limitations of our physical existence is to build constructs of holiness, both within ourselves and in the world around us. The first step is to set aside a place

---

22. See Ramban, *Devarim* 33:16; Midrash *Lekach Tov, Shemot* 3:2.

of holiness, a sanctuary, in our hearts. We can begin only when we take the time and make the effort to discern what is holy and enter into it, partake of it, without the cynicism and political correctness that causes modern man to value all things equally. Some things are, in fact, better, truer, more holy than others, and these are the things—times, places, objects—that allow us to step into holiness. When we partake of holiness, we connect with what is beyond our limited physical existence. Holiness is our connection with the Eternal, and holiness, like the burning bush, is never consumed.

Parashat Tetzaveh
Searching for a Heart of Gold

Clothes can do many things; they can express a mood or serve as camouflage, attract attention, even seduce. Clothes can both conceal and reveal who we are. In this *parashah* the clothes of the newly-appointed High Priest are described in unusual detail. These clothes were stunning; the combination of colors and precious metals created a collage that expressed the importance of the clothes themselves, and presumably of the person wearing them. These clothes were both ornamental and ceremonial, laden with precious gems and metals, and we might wonder how such opulence is commensurate with the spiritual nature of the High Priest's mission.

Throughout history, there have been contenders for this exalted position and the trappings that are its hallmark. In fact, the rabbinic tradition regarding Korach's rebellion emphasizes that Korach coveted Aharon's garments as well as his job. Korach, we are told, complained that Aharon strutted about, dressed like "a bride on her wedding day"; apparently, that is precisely the kind of preening Korach desired.[23] His fixation on the garments was part of a narcissistic fantasy: He wanted to be no less than the center of attention. He wanted to be dressed in the beautiful clothes. This may have been the motivation in another episode recounted in the Talmud of a man who approached Hillel the

---

23. *B'midbar Rabbah* 18:4.

81

Elder and asked that he facilitate his conversion to Judaism—but only on condition that he would become the High Priest.

What was the nature of this clothing? Was it considered magical, or was it simply a sort of uniform, intended to set apart the High Priest from all others, lending the wearer the authority and power of office? Rabbinic teachings stress that the priestly garments had symbolic significance that was part and parcel of their appearance. The garments were an integral part of the job of the High Priest, and when they were worn by the person worthy of them, the clothes themselves brought about forgiveness for many of the indiscretions of which the nation was guilty.

First and foremost among these special garments was a vest, worn on the heart, which bore the names of the twelve tribes. Careful consideration of this vest reveals the secret of the clothes, the man who wore them, and the task with which he was entrusted.

At the burning bush, God revealed Himself to Moshe, and tasked him with a job that seemed to Moshe to be far beyond his own capabilities. Moshe pointed out his own inadequacies, but God reassured him that He Himself would see to it that the mission would be successful, and that, in addition, Moshe would be assisted by his brother Aharon. In fact, God told Moshe, Aharon was already on his way to meet him, "happy in his heart" that his younger brother Moshe had been chosen for greatness (*Shemot* 2:14). This was no polite smile or superficial social gesture; this was an authentic emotion from the depth of his being, attested to by God Himself. Coming after the entire book of *Bereishit*, in which it seems brothers can never get along, we are relieved when Moshe and Aharon are joyfully reunited, when Aharon feels no jealousy or resentment that his younger brother has been chosen, or that he himself has been cast in a supporting role. He feels only happiness for Moshe, and is more than willing to play a secondary role in the mission that lies ahead.

This was the greatness of Aharon. We may say that he had a heart of gold: He loved and respected his younger brother, and rejoiced in Moshe's success. In fact, he loved all of his "brothers" and "sisters," and did his utmost to assist them in any way he could. This went beyond his immediate family; Aharon considered the entire nation his extended family, his brothers and sisters, and in his heart they were all precious, holy, and immensely valuable.

The selection of Aharon for the unique position of High Priest was, therefore, a natural choice. Aharon never saw his job as the expression of his own needs or desires; he consistently put the needs of his family first. Aharon mastered the art of thinking and feeling in the plural. He thought in terms of "we," not "I," which is why he was uniquely capable of wearing the precious stones and gold of the priestly vest on his heart: He wore them as an expression not of his own ego and needs, but as a representation of the entire Jewish people. He wore on his heart a mirror, as it were, of what he felt in his heart. He did not wear clothes that glorified him; he basked in the clothing that expressed the holiness and preciousness of his brothers and sisters, and carried the weight of their spiritual and physical wellbeing in—and on—his heart. When Aharon entered the sanctuary, he never entered as an individual. He represented the dreams and aspirations, the holiness and sanctity, as well as the shortcomings and failures, of the entire nation. He prayed, from the depths of his heart, for forgiveness for the nation—a nation that was nothing more or less than his own extended family, whose names were inscribed on the vest on his heart. Only a man with a heart of gold, a heart that was filled with happiness by the success of others, could be capable of wearing such clothing.

Parashat Ki Tisa
The View From Above

Of all the elements of the sin of the Golden Calf, the most striking is the stark contrast: Moshe stands on the top of the mountain, in the stratosphere both physically and spiritually, about to receive the Torah, while at the foot of the mountain the people sink to the lowest possible level, rebelling against every religious, social and spiritual norm.

It is the split-screen that haunts us; those who stand below are involved in such demeaning behavior that we imagine they must have been oblivious to the goings on above. If we overlay our mental image of these two scenes with appropriate background music, the contrast is brought into even sharper focus: Above, Moshe's rendezvous with God might be accompanied by the softest, most angelic and harmonic sounds—perhaps a heavenly harp or the most sublime violin concerto. At the foot of the mountain, we might expect to hear rhythmic, tribal drums piercing the air, whipping the people into recklessness, egging them on to join in the orgiastic frenzy (perhaps the Rolling Stones' "Sympathy for the Devil" might capture the mood).

The contrast is heartbreaking; we read with bated breath, hoping that they will come to their senses, break the trance they are in, and lift their eyes up for even a brief glance, and remember what is going on just above them. The contrast reminds us of some of the worst human behaviors in the most intimate relationships: A wife cheats on her husband as he sits in the bank, arranging the mortgage for their dream home. A husband cheats on his wife as she goes into labor and is trying to make her way to the hospital. It is the contrast of dedication versus infidelity, commitment versus mayhem, love versus lust, building a relationship versus seeking instant gratification, eternity versus immediacy, body versus soul, animal instinct versus human decency.

Stark contrast such as this does not just "happen": In order to sin, one must become completely unaware of what takes place above, beyond oneself. Only the conscious turning away, averting one's gaze from heaven, allows this behavior. At Mount Sinai, the first step is the removal of Moshe; in their minds, he is dead. Once free of their external "superego" the people are at liberty to walk on the wild side, to allow the "id" to run wild. Moshe is no longer there to scold them, and they allow themselves to live in the moment, and degrade themselves in the process.

Of course, Moshe is quite alive. Not only is he still at the peak of Sinai, he takes up their pathetic case and argues like the bravest defense attorney for his client—a client who is in fact impossibly guilty and without merit. Had he rejected them in disgust we would have understood his position; his defense of this primitive people is as surprising as it is uplifting. And yet, Moshe speaks with conviction. He knows that they are capable of more. He is convinced that they have, in the depths of their collective identity, decency that will yet emerge. Moshe is convinced that this is a people that has not yet peaked, a people with greatness in its future. Moshe believes in the Jewish People, and their ability to have a healthy relationship with God, a relationship of fidelity and reciprocal love.

And this brings us to the second point: While man lives below without thought of what is taking place above, while he puts thoughts of heaven out of his mind in order to sin, what saves him from himself and his own sin is the events in heaven. At the exact moment that they bow to the golden calf and muster up every last ounce of their energy to block out all thoughts of God and Moshe, purposefully averting their gaze from the peak of the mountain, it is precisely the conversation taking place on the peak of the mountain that saves them from obliteration. As the outrage reaches a crescendo, the forgotten and rejected Moshe prays to a forgotten and rejected God on behalf of a people with a very short memory and limited faith. The truly amazing thing is that God accepts the prayer: God, too, ultimately believes in the Jewish People, and is willing to overlook their indiscretion and continue to build a relationship with them.

Did these people—do we—ever take a moment to consider what occurred in heaven while we behaved so badly down below? Perhaps if we did, we would not need a Moshe to scold us. We would be simply too embarrassed to sin again. Did this contrast, the "split-screen" image of those critical hours and days, ever become as apparent to them as it should be to us? Perhaps focusing on the split-screen contrast might help bring our condition into focus, highlighting for us the absurdity of averting our eyes from what goes on beyond ourselves. Adopting the perspective of the loftier, more holy side of that split screen, as opposed to the clouded, limited perspective of the other half, is surely the key to living a holier life.

Parashat Vayakhel
(Constructive) Creativity

Parashat Vayakhel finds us in the midst of the construction of the Sanctuary, the Mishkan, and contains precise instructions for the select and elite group of artisans that will create the Mishkan itself, the objects it will house, and the ritual garments. In the midst of these highly detailed descriptions, Moshe gathers the people to give them instruction concerning Shabbat. Although this is not the first discussion of Shabbat, one particular prohibition is singled out in this *parashah*'s treatment that is not found elsewhere.

Generally, the Torah does not spell out specific activities that are prohibited on Shabbat; the scriptural treatment of Shabbat is largely generic, aimed at creating the philosophical framework for its observance. The particulars of the Laws of Shabbat, the 39 categories of creative activity that are proscribed on the weekly day of rest, are transmitted mainly through the Oral Tradition. Rabbinic tradition teaches us that the underpinnings for all of the laws regarding creative activity on Shabbat are learned from the context created by *Parashat Vayakhel*: Because the particulars of the Laws of Shabbat are transmitted in the context of the building of the Mishkan, a line is drawn between the work of the various artisans that would create and furnish the Mishkan, and the activities from which we refrain in observance of Shabbat.[24]

---

24. Talmud Bavli *Shabbat* 70a.

The parallel that this juxtaposition creates goes beyond the basic categories of creative endeavor: It implies a parallel between God's creation of the world and man's ability to give testimony to that creation as well as to produce a microcosm of that creation through the building of the Mishkan.

The opening verses of *Parashat Vayakhel* are true to this general method, as they present the concept of the six day work-week and the seriousness of the prohibition against creative labor on Shabbat. The statement that is tacked on to this somewhat familiar formula seems uncharacteristically detailed, singling out the prohibition against the active use of fire on the Sabbath. This specific prohibition is best understood in terms of the broader underpinnings of Shabbat as a microcosm or imitation of God's creation of the universe. *Bereishit* recounts the origins of creation, first in the general statement, "In the beginning God created the heaven and the earth," and then with the specific act of creation: "Let there be light." In much the same fashion, we are commanded in a general sense to observe Shabbat, and then immediately commanded to desist from using the creative force of fire. In a very real sense, our use of fire, our ability to harness energy, is the primary manifestation that man is created in the image of God. In echoing the dramatic call, "Let there be light," we may even delude ourselves into believing that we, too, are gods. The fact that we do not make creative use of this power on Shabbat allows us to regain our perspective, to readjust our sights, and to reconnect with the Creator.

However, the creative activities from which we refrain on Shabbat do more than readjust the playing field in terms of our relationship with God. The laws of Shabbat also serve as great democratizers, allowing us to readjust our social perspective as well. One prohibition in particular, the prohibition against carrying or transferring material from one location to another, poignantly illustrates this aspect of Jewish law.

In a sense, these two activities—harnessing the power of fire and transporting objects from place to place—seem almost diametric opposites. The former stands at the forefront of human achievement, transforming both the object to which it is applied and our lives in general; the latter simply transports but does not transform. Moving an object does not alter it in any way, and hardly seems creative. In fact, Rabbeinu Tam, one of the great sages of the Middle Ages, categorized carrying an object (or transferring it from one domain to another) as a "weak creative activity."[25]

When I studied these laws with the late Rabbi Yosef Dov Soloveitchik, he remarked that they reminded him of the history of Europe's trade unions. When the trade unions began organizing almost a century ago, artisans' guilds strongly opposed the inclusion of those involved in transport—carriage and wagon-train drivers, mule-team leaders, as well as railroad workers and, much later, truckers. The skilled, "creative" professionals, many of whom practiced trades that had been handed down for generations, were not inclined to consider the "non-creative" movers as equally deserving of representation and protection. Rabbi Soloveitchik compared this approach to Rabbeinu Tam's description of the halachic category of carrying objects on Shabbat as "weak creative activity" that is nonetheless prohibited on Shabbat.

And herein lies the great democratizing effect of the laws of Shabbat: The activities that stand at the apex of creative activity—using fire to cook or forge, writing or erasing written words, planting or harvesting, dyeing, spinning or sewing— are equal, in the eyes of Shabbat observance, to the "weakest" creative activity, in which an object is moved from one place

---

25. Tosafot *Shevuot* 2a, s.v. *yetziot ha-Shabbat shtayim she-heim arba*; Tosafot *Shabbat* 2a, s.v. *pashat ba'al ha-bayit et yado,* this same teaching is reported in the name of Rabbeinu Yitzchak.

to another. In creating the Mishkan, the skilled artisans were involved in the creation of the holy objects and the Sanctuary—and the movers and construction laborers were equally involved. Their contribution was valued, their task no less holy. Similarly, in the eyes of Jewish law, production, transport and delivery are all links in the chain of commerce, and are therefore equally proscribed on Shabbat. The day of rest applies equally to every laborer and every type of creative labor. Just as every Jew had a part in the Mishkan, so every Jew has a part in the holiness of Shabbat.

Parashat Pekudei
A Happy Ending

As we arrive at the end of the Book of *Shemot*, we are left with mixed feelings. On the one hand, the book seems to have a happy ending. Any reader who appreciates the hopelessness of the situation of the Israelite slaves in Egypt as they are described in the book's early chapters, and contrasts their plight with the end of the book, where the people are free and spiritually attuned, must declare *Shemot* an exceptional narrative of liberation, a victorious *tour de force*.

Reading through the book in more detail would most likely lead the reader to the same conclusion: The book of *Shemot* is a success story, describing an unparalleled, epic march from slavery to salvation, from redemption to revelation. The hated, obstinate Pharaoh and his sadistic henchmen are punished, measure for measure: Their cruelty and arrogance lead them to the bottom of the sea. The Jews march to Sinai, witness the most glorious theophany in human history, and build a sanctuary in which this singular revelation can be recalled, recast and repeated on a daily basis. *Shemot* ends as the Glory of God fills the Mishkan, in the midst of this unique nation.

Surely, as might be expected, there were some setbacks—small "mini-rebellions," a degree of grumbling and complaining, a minor "military action," and even one glaring, glistening, golden transgression. But surely, by the end of the book, all has been forgiven and forgotten. Or has it?

This is the question that gnaws at us: Was this, in fact, the way the book was supposed to end? At first glance, the question seems absurd: What better final chapter could we have hoped for? The Glory of God Himself had descended into the completed Mishkan. The entire camp was transformed into a place of holiness, like no other known to mankind. The Children of Israel stood poised to continue their journey, to fulfill their destiny.

And therein lies the rub: This entire generation will never make it to the Promised Land. Likewise, their leader Moshe will never step foot in the "land flowing with milk and honey."

As originally scripted, the "screenplay" was quite different: After a short stopover at Sinai, where the people would gain the spiritual focus and energy that would carry them forward to their final destination, Moshe should have led the glorious march that ended in Jerusalem. There, the Presence of God would have filled the newly-built Temple, the Beit HaMikdash, the eternal seat of God on earth. The Word of God should have rung out from Jerusalem, as teachings of decency, peace and freedom began, first as a ripple but soon as a tidal wave of righteousness, to sweep across and enlighten the world. The inhabitants of the land would have bowed their heads, acknowledging that the rightful owners had come home; they would have handed them the keys and politely excused themselves.

But this is not how the book ends. In fact, the entire scenario never came to fruition—not for Moshe's generation, nor for any other. The entire generation that experienced the great miracles described throughout *Shemot*, all the adults who entered into the Covenant at Sinai, perished in the desert, as did Moshe.

If we read the last chapters of *Shemot* while considering what should have been, the ending of the book is a bittersweet tale of missed opportunity. What we thought was a story of triumph becomes a description of failure. *Shemot* concludes as the temporary temple, the Tabernacle or Mishkan, is consecrated. In fact, the Mishkan should never have existed; it is but a cheap imitation of what was meant to be. Clearly, had the building of the permanent Temple, the Beit HaMikdash in Jerusalem, not been delayed, there would have been no need for a temporary construct that would accompany them on their travels through the wilderness. The forty-year sojourn in the desert was not a part of the original plan; it was a result of those "little rebellions" and that golden calf. In fact, our bad choices had far more impact than we might care to consider. Those choices forced a detour—geographical, chronological and spiritual—that led us so far away from our goal that even after millennia we have not achieved it.

Was the building of the Mishkan a pyrrhic victory? Are there times in our own lives when we do the same—celebrate what we think is a great accomplishment, without realizing that we are actually settling for a mere shadow of what could or should have been? Do we settle for spiritually inferior accomplishments, basking in their modest glory while stunting our imagination, not allowing ourselves to strive higher, to envision our souls, and indeed the entire world, perfected?

The Book of *Shemot* has come to an end, yet the story it should have recorded remains untold. The mission remains unfinished. We are charged with taking up the vision of what should have been, and seeing it through. In order to do so, we must liberate our minds from the artificial boundaries we have imposed upon ourselves, and envision a world elevated and free, a world in which the story of the Exodus finally reaches its glorious intended conclusion.

ספר
ויקרא

Parashat Vayikra
Intimacy

The Book of *Vayikra* opens with a peculiar turn of phrase: "And [He] called out to Moshe, and God spoke to him." Apparently, as readers, we were unaware that the Book of *Shemot* came to an abrupt end, in mid-sentence. For that matter, we are not necessarily aware that we are reading the continuation of the story as we begin the Book of *Vayikra*. Only when we consider the Book of *Vayikra* as the continuation of *Shemot* and read them contiguously do we begin to grasp the connection.

To be sure, God calling out to man—especially to Moshe—is not an unusual occurrence in the Torah; nonetheless, the opening verse of *Vayikra* is different. Now, God calls out from within the completed Temple. To fully understand this difference we need context. Reading *Vayikra* in the context of the final verses of *Shemot* helps us to understand that *Vayikra* is not merely the continuation of the Book of Exodus—it is the culmination of the Exodus itself. A metaphor found in the book of Jeremiah helps us gain greater insight into the story:

> Go and proclaim in the ears of Jerusalem, saying, "Thus says God: I remember the kindness of your youth, your love as a bride, how you followed Me in the wilderness, in a land that was not sown" (Jeremiah 2:2).

God reminisces fondly about the early days of His relationship with the Jewish People: In Egypt, the Jews were like a damsel in distress, liberated by a "knight in shining armor." After He rescues them, they follow their savior off into the desert "like a love-sick bride," to their rendezvous at Sinai.

Standing at Sinai, vows are exchanged, and Moshe goes up to bring down the tablets of stone, a symbol of their unique and exclusive relationship (analogous to a wedding ring), to complete the marriage ceremony. At that precise moment, havoc is unleashed. The erstwhile lovesick bride gets cold feet; she backs away from her commitment and indulges in a fling, seeking thrills with a cheap imitation of her betrothed. At this point, talk of marriage seems absurd; the possibility of a life together seems to have vanished into thin air. Nonetheless Moshe intercedes, and soon the relationship is back on track. There is regret, repentance, and the relationship is repaired. Moshe ascends the mountain once again, and brings a second ring. They build a home, a place in which their love can be expressed, experienced and nurtured.

The Book of *Shemot* comes to a close as the building is completed. The structure stands, ready to embody and facilitate their unique relationship. Only one thing is missing: intimacy. And that is what the Book of *Vayikra* is about: intimacy with God, which may also be called "holiness." Certainly God has spoken to Moshe many times; Moshe even went up Mount Sinai and met with God at the summit. But this is different; now, man has made place for God down on earth. There is now an aspect of permanence to this relationship. A home has been built for them to share. Up to this point, the romance has been beautiful and uplifting: It is certainly an exalted gesture for man to lift himself toward the heavens and try to connect to the holiness above, but it is quite another matter to bring the holiness to this world. This new stage of the relationship requires constancy, commitment of a totally different order. For their relationship to fully blossom, they must shift from the sensation of being swept away by a love affair, and begin to nurture and maintain that love in a constant, ongoing and stable relationship of commitment and attentiveness.

This is what the Book of *Vayikra* is about, and it is the message of the very first verse. While the previous book ended with a completed house for God, *Vayikra* begins as the voice of God calls out to Moshe from inside the house. Holiness has been successfully brought down to earth; now, the world "below" has a chance to be elevated. Now the bride and groom can start their life together, in the home they have built for their shared future. Now, intimacy begins.

Parashat Tzav
Impetuousness

As the Mishkan (Sanctuary) is about to become operational, one last detail must be addressed: Aharon and his sons must go through a process whereby they will become *kohanim* (priests). In addition to various rituals that will prepare them for their new position, a seven-day period of confinement is commanded, during which time the initiates are not to leave the Mishkan. We might describe these days as the "cooling off" period necessary for the transition from civilian life to the holy life of the *kohen*, yet the specific duration of this period of confinement seems to contain allusions to other contexts.

At various junctures, the Jewish People as a whole, and specific, particular individuals, were commanded to undergo transformative preparatory rituals in order to achieve a new level of holiness or a more elevated spiritual status. However, only in certain cases was a full seven days mandated: In the case perhaps most germane to the topic at hand, the Torah tells us that the High Priest (*Kohen Gadol*) is also separated for seven days in preparation for Yom Kippur. He leaves his home, his wife and family, and spends seven days in a state of spiritual, intellectual, and physical preparation for the crucial task he will perform on the Day of Atonement. Similarly, the *kohen* who is appointed to prepare the Red Heifer, the instrument through which the people achieve ritual cleansing after any contact with death, is also separated for seven days in preparation for his holy task. While we might argue that the common denominator of all three instances of separation is simply a dedication of time in preparation for an exalted task, there may be a much deeper, more intrinsic connection between them.

Each of these three instances—the Mishkan, Yom Kippur, and the Red Heifer—creates spiritual healing. The Mishkan was built in order to create a place to which any and all in need of spiritual repair could turn. Yom Kippur was set aside for all time as the most efficacious day of the year for healing communal and personal sins. The purpose of the Red Heifer is to purify after contact with death, which creates a spiritual malady that only a spiritual process can heal. In each case, the Torah outlines rituals designed to bring man close to God. Apparently, in order to achieve this closeness, a seven-day separation from normal life is required. But why? Why the separation, and why is an entire week mandated for these particular processes?

Often, sin is the result of man pursuing his basest impulses, eschewing the divine image within him, averting his gaze from God, and instead choosing to follow his animal instinct. This may not seem like a "choice"; it is not the result of careful contemplation but of "spontaneous combustion," of a momentary lapse of clear thinking in which impetuousness wins. Consequences are not considered, implications and ramifications are ignored, resulting in sin—or death. For this reason, the process through which the *kohen* is readied for his task is not simply a waiting period. It is part of an intellectual and spiritual process of maturation, as it were, in which he is weaned from impulsive behavior.

An essential aspect of the *kohen*'s service is *kavanah*—intent or directed thought. If the *kohen* misdirects his focus while performing the ritual, even if every possible detail of the prescribed rite is performed with absolute precision, the service is invalidated. The smallest stray thought of partaking of the offering at the wrong time or place, for example, nullifies the entire offering.

It is for this reason that a period of separation is mandated. It allows the *kohen* an opportunity to recalibrate, to gain control over his thoughts and, by extension, his actions. This "quarantine" reduces distractions to a minimum, creating a sort of funnel through which he may concentrate his attention, focus and direct his thoughts, and take full control of his intellectual and spiritual capabilities in order to master the physical, instinctual parts of his personality.

Another instance of a seven-day period of separation involves Moshe's preparation to ascend Mount Sinai for an experience that would change the Jewish People, and in fact all of mankind. At Mount Sinai, the Jewish People come of age, as it were: At the moment the Torah is received, mankind achieves a new level of spiritual and intellectual maturity, a level that puts them in touch with their inner greatness, their inner divinity. From that moment hence, the Torah will constitute the charter of the newly-born nation and its moral, ethical and legal code. From this point on, they will be held accountable for their actions and responsible for their personal and communal conduct, rather than being ruled by instinct or impulse. As their capacity to control their animal instincts develops, their souls change, grow, flourish. When they fail, as they inevitably do, sin—even death—can and must be cleansed, healed. Focus and equilibrium must be regained through the triumph of the soul over the body.

The rehabilitative process is a personal journey, but it is facilitated by the *kohen*. Like any mentor, the *kohen* must undergo this same process of spiritual redirection in order to be a useful and effective guide. Indeed, the *kohen*'s journey takes the process one step further, teaching us that man has the capacity not only to abandon impetuous, instinctive behavior, but to transform it into a something new: Instinctual behavior based on devotion and self-sacrifice.

This was the *kohen*'s mandate, and it continues to define Jewish leadership to this very day. How else can we explain the behavior of Major Ro'i Klein, a soldier and scholar who, upon seeing a grenade hurled at the soldiers under his charge, commanded them to take cover as he jumped upon the grenade, taking the full impact of the blast? The last words on his lips were the *Shema*, the declaration of unwavering confidence in the unity of God and His unique relationship with the Jewish People. With the holiness of a *Kohen Gadol*, he knowingly plunged into the crucible in order to save others. Yes, he acted instinctively, impulsively—but his instincts were not those of base physical survival. He had achieved an elevated and purified level of instinct that others before him throughout our history achieved, a dedication to God and to the Jewish People that are born of the focus and attention—*kavanah*—to which we are all commanded to aspire. Each of us is capable of transforming our instincts, elevating them to the level of holiness.

Parashat Shmini
Separations

As it becomes operational, the Mishkan (Tabernacle) engenders new responsibilities: Aharon is commanded to abstain from intoxicating beverages as he is called upon to function as *kohen*. At first glance, this prohibition appears to be a practical precaution against the debilitating effects of alcohol and the diminished capacity often associated with drinking. There are, however, rabbinic traditions that read this commandment as ominous foreshadowing, linking it with the sudden, tragic deaths of Aharon's two sons on that very same day. According to this view, Nadav and Avihu were intoxicated when they approached the Mishkan on the eighth day of its consecration, and the results of their impaired judgment were fatal.

Despite this alternative reading, we need look no further than the Torah text itself to understand the new commandment given to the *kohanim*. In somewhat unusual form, the Torah offers an explanation of the inner workings of this prohibition: "To separate between the holy and the mundane and between the impure and the pure." When properly understood, this commandment speaks to the very core of the Mishkan, and for that matter, the entire book of *Vayikra*.

While *Vayikra* begins with the completed Mishkan and the laws that will frame and enable the service of the *kohanim*, the focus and scope of *Vayikra's* legal purview quickly expand to encompass each and every Jew, in all areas of life, to include such matters as permitted and forbidden foods, as well as permitted and forbidden sexual partners. In each of these cases, the legal precept is described as creating a "separation."

The commandments transmitted in the book of *Vayikra* are not the first mention of the concept of "separation." In the Torah's opening verses, the creation of the world is described as a process of separation—between darkness and light, between water and water. By definition, separation indicates distinction, but is not necessarily indicative of a value judgment. The separations through which our physical reality was created may be understood in terms of utility, and we may easily imagine that the Torah could have described the Divine act of Creation without employing the terminology of separation.

In the description of creation, the only use of the concept of holiness was in the context of Shabbat, the day that commemorates the acts of separation through which God created the universe. On the other hand, in the process of creating the Mishkan, the concept of holiness is the dominant theme, but up to this point, no explicit mention has been made of the concept of separation. Only now, as the unique commandments regarding Aharon's comportment in the Mishkan are recorded, the cross-pollination of these ideas comes to fruition. The Mishkan, a construct dedicated to holiness, is a microcosm of a new world, a world in which mankind can access holiness. Therefore, when man is called upon to build the Mishkan, inherent in the process is a series of acts of separation that lead to a state of holiness.

One of the most axiomatic concepts taught by our sages is that holiness means separateness.[26] To be holy is to acknowledge, to internalize and to act upon concepts of separation and separateness, gradations and seemingly slight differences that permeate and define time, space, and matter. In this *parashah*,

---

26. See Ramban, *Vayikra* 19:2, *Sifra Kedoshim parashah* 1.

the vehicle through which the Torah conveys these concepts points our attention toward the need for clarity regarding these delicate separations: *Kohanim* must not drink wine before serving in the Mishkan.

The mystical tradition teaches that the Tree of Knowledge of Good and Evil—the tree at the center of the Garden of Eden whose fruit causes confusion and leads to death—was a grapevine. When fermented, the fruit of this tree intoxicates and confuses us, and leads us to overstep boundaries, to overlook the subtle separations that create holiness. In this respect, the tragic story of the deaths of Aharon's sons, and the prohibition against drinking by the *kohen*—both of which emphasize "separation"—serve as an introduction to the entire book of *Vayikra*.

The creation of holiness causes unavoidable collateral damage, for only when we become aware of the holy can we become sensitive to what remains outside the parameters of holiness. The creation of holiness gives rise, unavoidably, to the profane. Whereas the amorphous condition of "unholiness" had been the *status quo ante*, only now, in sharp distinction to the radiant, uplifted state of holiness does the unholy suddenly seem dark and dreary. Before there is holiness, there cannot, by definition, be "unholiness." Therefore, only as the Mishkan becomes functional, these concepts of separation and holiness come into focus, but like the scope of the book of *Vayikra*, the implications of these concepts reach every aspect of our lives and allow us to reach new levels of spiritual perfection.

Parashat Tazria
Seclusion

Tum'ah is a word that is not easily defined. While we use the word "impurity" to translate the concept of *tum'ah*, modern man has very little grasp of ritual purity and impurity. Although we share the dread caused by the most feared source of impurity—death—it is death itself we fear, and not the state of ritual impurity it causes.

Death is modern man's ultimate fear. It is the ultimate defeat; it debilitates not only the victim, but also those left behind—loved ones, family and friends. And yet, in our experience, when death makes an appearance, the *tum'ah* that results is "healed" by a simple washing of the hands; a few cups of water and life goes on—at least in terms of *tum'ah*. In Temple times, however, a person who had come in contact with death could not enter the Temple; *tum'ah* and the sanctity of the Temple are mutually exclusive concepts. For the same reason, all *kohanim*, whose lives were intimately intertwined with the Temple service, were commanded to avoid unnecessary contact with the dead. Even today, *kohanim* attend funerals only for their most immediate relatives, and actively avoid all contact with death except when absolutely necessary.

In short, we have little difficulty understanding the concept of *tum'ah* that has death at its source. And yet, despite the tragedy of death, the permanent and irreversible damage and void that it creates and the dread of its cruel finality, there is another type of *tum'ah* that is far worse: the *tum'ah* of *tzara'at*. Our sages explain that the malady called *tzara'at*, commonly translated as leprosy, is not the physical skin malady with which we are familiar, but rather a physical expression of a spiritual illness.

At first glance, death—and the *tum'ah* it engenders— seems to us far more serious and severe than any skin lesion; in fact, *tzara'at* might even seem trivial compared to death. Nonetheless, when we measure and compare the *tum'ah* that results from each of these causes, the conclusion is inescapable: The *tum'ah* caused by leprosy eclipses that caused by contact with death. The verses themselves illustrate the disparity: A person who came in contact with death could not enter the Temple, but the leper was completely removed from society. While we might argue that the quarantine of the leper was nothing more than a preventative step to avoid contagion—a step that is unnecessary in the case of *tum'ah* caused by contact with death—this argument overlooks the nature of *tum'ah*. The malady in question is spiritual, not physical. The leper is placed in isolation because he or she suffers from a contagious condition that is spiritual, not physical.

Tradition associates leprosy with sins of speech, such as gossip, slander and character assassination.[27] The person guilty of these sins is considered spiritually dangerous, and the results of these sins are considered far more destructive than contact with death.

The first instance of the misuse of speech was in the Garden of Eden, and it was perpetrated by the serpent. In attempting to bring about disharmony between Adam and Eve, the serpent serves as the prototype of the gossiper who sows hatred and jealousy through the artful use of words. With its slick message and scaly skin, the serpent has become the quintessential image of the misuse of speech—and of the skin lesions that result.

---

27. Talmud Bavli *Erchin* 15b.

As a result of the serpent's insidious words, mankind's grasp of truth was confounded, confused; they were exiled from the Garden of Eden. After partaking of the Tree of Knowledge of Good and Evil—a tree we might more aptly call the "Tree of Death"—they were banished, exiled, distanced from the Garden and the intimacy with God they had once enjoyed, the source of life itself. As God had warned, death came into the world. And so, we begin to see that the circle is complete: The serpent, and all those who misuse the power of speech, create a spiritual wound in human society—a wound whose physical manifestation may be likened to the skin of the snake. This condition is called *tzara'at*, and it results from the same sin committed by the serpent in the Garden of Eden. Any person who behaves like the serpent must be banished, sent into temporary exile, to protect society from infection while allowing the sinner to be healed spiritually.

Slander, gossip, and other serpent-like abuses of the gift of speech bring a type of spiritual death into the community, just as the serpent's misuse of speech brought physical death into the world. In both cases, the *tum'ah* necessarily results in estrangement, exile—either from the Temple or from all of society. And though in both cases a type of death occurs, *Parashat Tazria* teaches us that spiritual death is by far the greater loss.

Parashat Metzora
Feeling Kinship

As the Torah continues its discussion of spiritual "leprosy," we learn that this strange malady can affect not only one's person, but also their clothing and their home. Though the laws in the Torah are taught in that order—person, clothing, home—rabbinic tradition teaches that the outbreak would take place in inverse order: First the home would be afflicted, then the clothing, and finally the person. The sequence is significant; it progresses from impersonal to personal, giving the sufferer various opportunities to discern the spiritual message and resolve to make amends.

Regarding the affliction of a house, the Torah prefaces the law with the qualification that it will apply "when you come to the land of Canaan" (14:34). Recognizing, as we do, that the malady in question is a physical manifestation of a spiritual ailment, we are not surprised that the law will apply only in the Land of Israel, where the nation will be expected to live a morally and spiritually exalted existence. What is surprising is that in this particular context, the Promised Land is referred to as "the land of Canaan." There is certainly no dearth of possibilities when referring to the Land of Israel; the Israelites' ultimate destination is variously referred to as the land promised to the patriarchs, or the land flowing with milk and honey, or even the land presently controlled by various other tribes. Why, specifically regarding the affliction of a home with *tzara'at*, does the Torah single out Canaan?

Rabbinic tradition addressed the laws regarding "leprosy" through the prism of spirituality, noting the connection between *tzara'at* and *tzarut 'ayin* (stinginess or miserliness of spirit).[28] In particular, we are taught that a person who turns down a neighbor's request to borrow a tool or utensil, claiming that he does not own the item in question simply because he does not wish to share, will be struck with *tzara'at*. The prescribed treatment for *tzara'at* that afflicts a house, outlined in *Parashat Metzora*, is to cast the contents of the leprous home out of doors, effectively placing all the miser's possessions on public display for all the rebuffed neighbors, relatives and friends to see.

And yet, the question remains: How does this relate to Canaan?

After the flood, Noach, ostensibly suffering from post-traumatic stress and perhaps some guilt for having survived while saving nary a soul, becomes intoxicated. His son Ham finds him lying naked and drunk on the floor, and seizes the opportunity to abuse his father. Noah's two remaining sons see this and respectfully cover their father while averting their eyes from his embarrassment.[29]

When Noah awakens from his alcohol-induced slumber and realizes what his son has done, his response is strange. Rather than responding to the outrage or disciplining Ham, Noah makes a very harsh pronouncement regarding Ham's son, Canaan. Apparently, this is not as much a curse as a statement of cause and effect: The son who showed no respect for his father will in turn know disrespect from his own son.

Honoring one's parents is the most basic and logical of interpersonal laws, and its "spill-over" effects are far-reaching: The son who respects his parents will, by extension, be kind to his siblings and their children as well. It is not difficult to

---

28. *B'midbar Rabbah* 7:5.
29. *Bereishit* 9:20-27.

see how this affects the dynamics of the entire Jewish People: We are one family, one fraternity; we are all brothers and sisters, hence our homes should be open to our neighbors, and our good fortune shared with a glad heart and spirit. This is what sets us apart from the descendants of Ham and his son Canaan, and it is this understanding of our familial responsibilities that causes the land occupied by Canaan to be given to the children of Shem through the line of Avraham: Only when we create a charitable and kind society, a society based on mutual responsibility, a society based on our sense of family, will we merit this inheritance. To behave like Ham or like Canaan, to turn our backs on our brothers and sisters, to be motivated by *tzarut 'ayin* rather than the *hesed* that is the hallmark of Avraham and Sarah's descendants, is an affront to the values of our forebears and to God Himself, as well as to the Land of Israel.

Parashat Aharei Mot
Rectification

The *parashah* begins with an ominous frame of reference: "After the deaths of the two sons of Aharon." The deaths of Nadav and Avihu are recounted earlier in the Book of *Vayikra*, although some five chapters, laden with commandments, separate the tragic events of day of the Tabernacle's consecration from the Torah's response to those events in our present *parashah*. In fact, the content of the commandments that are transmitted in this *parashah* may be regarded as no less ominous than the events that frame them: In this chapter, God conveys the laws that constitute the Yom Kippur service. The Day of Atonement, first instituted here, will be a constant in Jewish life for all time, yet this first Yom Kippur must have raised mixed feelings for Aharon. On the one hand, Yom Kippur marks the day that Moshe obtained forgiveness from God for the sin of the golden calf; on the other hand, Aharon played no small part in that sin.

We find ourselves at a strange intersection of the two great tragedies in Aharon's life: the deaths of his children and the sin of the golden calf. One wonders if the thought ever crossed his mind that these events might be connected.

From our perspective, the Yom Kippur ritual seems to contain echoes of both of these tragedies. The sin committed by Nadav and Avihu that led to their deaths was bringing incense that they were not commanded to bring. Conversely, the climactic moment of the Yom Kippur service is the entry of the High Priest into the Holy of Holies to ignite the incense and create a cloud, as per the precise instructions recorded in this *parashah*. On Yom Kippur, this cloud and the scent it carries somehow facilitate forgiveness, whereas in the case of Aharon's sons, the result was the polar opposite.

A cloud of a different kind was a central aspect of the Revelation at Sinai. The cloud was a visual representation of God Himself descending, as it were, to the physical plane in order to rendezvous with His people and give them the Torah. Later, Moshe ascended into the cloud to bring down the Tablets of Stone, the physical testament to the Revelation. While Moshe was at the summit of Mount Sinai, the sin of the golden calf unfolded; as a result, the Tablets were shattered. Thus, in a very real sense, the giving of the Torah, the completion of the process that began as the cloud descended on the mountain, was "ruined" by the golden calf. The cloud dissipated, as did the protective clouds that had accompanied the Israelites as they left Egypt. Only on the tenth day of Tishrei, precisely one year before the events recorded in *Parashat Aharei Mot*, on the day that would become known as Yom Kippur, the people were forgiven and Moshe was given a new set of Tablets, and as a result, the clouds which protected the Jewish people soon returned. Now, on that same date one year later, Aharon and his descendants are commanded to recreate the cloud, to enter the Holy of Holies in a cloud of incense. This cloud, on this day, will effectuate forgiveness.

In the Yom Kippur ritual, God elegantly addressed both failings: By commanding Aharon to bring incense, God instructed Aharon to do what his sons had done, with one crucial difference: They had now received a commandment. There would be no free-style, spontaneous worship; approaching the holiest place on earth would be permitted only through precise adherence to the Word of God. At the same time, the cloud of incense would recreate the atmosphere at Mount Sinai on the day the Torah was first given. Yom Kippur captures both the exalted moment before the sin of the golden calf and the day the Torah was finally received—the day God forgave them for their terrible transgression and Moshe descended with the second Tablets of Testimony.

This same day becomes, for all time, a day on which we can return to a more pure state, cleanse ourselves of our sins, and make a new commitment to accepting God's commandments—which is the very core of repentance, the very essence of the day. God even accepts our clumsy, misguided attempts to relate to Him by transforming those very same actions into commandments that lie at the heart of the Day of Atonement, creating the dynamic that recasts our sins as *mitzvot*.

By commanding Aharon to do precisely what his sons had done—to recreate the cloud of Revelation and seek out intimacy with the Divine—God allows each and every one of us to experience that intimacy every Yom Kippur. When we approach this intermingling of holiness and intimacy properly, even the most profound transgressions can be forgiven.

Parashat Kedoshim
In Search of Holiness

As *Parashat Kedoshim* begins, Moshe is instructed to assemble the entire community for a public reading of a specific set of laws. The stated purpose of this assembly is to achieve holiness. This exercise should be considered in light of a statement found in the previous *parashah* which serves as the backdrop or background for what will follow: In order for the enterprise we call "Judaism" to be sustained in the Promised Land, a different standard of decency will be required. Israel is a holy land, and it will not tolerate certain behaviors; its delicate constitution will literally "vomit out" indecency.

The specific laws that are to be read at this public gathering bear a striking similarity to the set of laws which were transmitted publicly, to the entire nation, at the foot of Mount Sinai—laws that came to be known as the Ten Commandments. Traditionally, the Ten Commandments, as a legal corpus, are considered the framework of Judaism's religious, social, and moral system. Far more than ten utterances of specific legislation, they are principles of law—principles that are expanded upon and applied in various ways in *Parashat Kedoshim*.

And yet, as important as the Ten Commandments are in defining Jewish mores and practice, there is another set of laws, introduced at the very dawn of creation, known as the Seven Noahide Laws.[30] The existence of this universal corpus explains

---

30. Talmud Bavli *Sanhedrin* 56a.

the seemingly odd fact that Judaism is not, nor has it ever been, a proselytizing religion. The Seven Noahide laws were given to all of mankind as a means to perfect humanity, while the more demanding and arduous strictures and limitations called for by Jewish law were never seen as obligatory for all of mankind.

Careful consideration of the Seven Noahide Laws reveals a fairly obvious correlation to the Ten Commandments. The Noahide Laws include creating a just legal system with a functioning judiciary, and the prohibition of idolatry, murder, theft, sexual immorality, blasphemy and eating the limb of a live animal. With the exception of latter, the overlap with the Ten Commandments is unmistakable. What is most striking, though, is what is *not* included in the Noahide laws: Honoring one's parents and Shabbat observance.

Although *shemirat Shabbat* (Sabbath observance) has become a benchmark for the Jewish religious experience, had non-Jews been ordered to commemorate the seventh day, and thus acknowledge God as the Creator of the universe, we would not have been surprised. Similarly, had the commandment to honor one's parents been bestowed upon all "Noahides," we would have no trouble grasping the universal importance of this law. Nonetheless, Noah and his descendants were not required to observe the Sabbath or to honor their parents.

Keeping this anomaly in mind, it is surely no coincidence that the very first laws that are to be read publicly at the assembly designed to create holiness in the Jewish polis, the laws that immediately follow the commandment to "be holy," are precisely the elements of the Ten Commandments that do not bind the Noahide: "Man shall have reverence for his mother and father, and guard my Sabbaths; I am God."

The context makes it clear: It is these particulars that are the core of holiness. Considered together, we may say that they

116

reflect a perspective that is unique to Judaism: While all the other laws deal with the present, only these elements deal with the past—Shabbat as a testimony to the creation of the universe, and reverence for parents who brought us into the world.

The Torah demands decency of the non-Jew; refraining from taking another's life, spouse or physical possessions is basic decency. However, the Torah does not require that the common man cultivate historical consciousness, a sense of where we came from or why we are here, who created us, who brought us into the world and who nurtured us. The laws that are unique to the Ten Commandments require us to keep a constant eye on the past, and this is a uniquely Jewish requirement that creates a uniquely Jewish perspective and experience.

Modern man, so full of hubris and an exaggerated sense of importance, looks at the past as being quaint, naïve, and barely relevant. Perhaps this is collateral damage of the belief in an evolutionary process in which one's ancestors were primates. In contrast, the elements of the Ten Commandments that are uniquely Jewish requirements teach us to look to the past as we move forward. Thus, no matter how sophisticated we become, the Sabbath remains relevant—perhaps even more than ever in a world of constant digital access and stimulation. The Torah teaches us that no matter how smart and important we think we have become, we must respect and cherish the previous generation, especially those who nurtured us, cared for us, gave us their unconditional love—and made our progress possible. The result of this perspective is a life steeped in holiness.

Parashat Emor
An Extension of Holiness

Centuries ago, a major argument shook the Jewish world.[31] The argument centered around the *omer* offering, specifically regarding the interpretation of the Torah passage commanding that the *omer* ceremony be performed "after the Shabbat." In context, the word *Shabbat* clearly refers to the Passover holiday, which is also a sabbatical day—a day of rest on which no labor is performed. Additionally, in an adjacent passage, both the first of Tishrei and the tenth of Tishrei are referred to as Shabbat. It is simply not possible that both of these dates would be Saturdays, being that there are only seven days in a week. Thus we must conclude, as did the mainstream rabbinic establishment of that time, that the term "Shabbat" means a day of rest, and not necessarily or exclusively "the Sabbath" in the classic sense of 'the seventh day of the week' (Saturday).

Unassailable as this logic may seem, during the Second Temple period there was nonetheless a group of Jews who insisted that the ceremony of the *omer* must always be performed literally "after Shabbat"—on a Saturday night. This group who fought the rabbis was known as the Boethusians.

At first glance the Boethusians seem to have espoused a more stringent form of religious adherence, particularly regarding Sabbath observance. In claiming that the *omer* must always be brought on a Saturday night, they ensured that this ritual,

31. Talmud Bavli *Menachot* 65a.

118

which involved harvesting grain, would never be performed on the Sabbath itself. On the other hand, mainstream rabbinic opinion allowed for the *omer* to be harvested and offered on whatever day of the week immediately followed the first day of Passover—hence, the *omer* ceremony would occasionally fall on the Sabbath. Despite the fact that this ceremony included going out to the field and harvesting some of the newly-grown barley, which would normally be labor that is prohibited on Shabbat, the rabbis felt that in the case of the *omer* offering—as in the case of all offerings brought in the Temple—the normal rules of Shabbat were held in abeyance. The Boethusians disagreed; in fact, their dissent was so strong that they went so far as to dispatch false witnesses to testify that they had seen the new moon in order to manipulate the calendar to align with their opinion.

The Boethusians' seemingly conservative approach to the sanctity of Shabbat actually masked a deeper issue: In their view, the Boethusians confined the concept of holiness to the Temple compound, while the rabbis' concept of *kedushah* extended to the most basic activities of everyday life. The rabbis believed that on occasion, even the fields, even the manual labor of harvesting barley, are holy. The rules that apply to the Temple and its exalted rites of sacrifice also pay a visit to the familiar agricultural milieu, creating *kedushah* that is so lofty as to supersede even the laws of Shabbat.

This distinction between the two opinions regarding the *omer* is no mere argument over minutiae of law; it reveals a vast chasm dividing two very different religious philosophies. Rabbinic Judaism regards the essence of Jewish life in the Land of Israel as an agricultural enterprise designed to bring holiness into every aspect of life. The field is not only a place of labor, it is a place of charity and social justice, where the poor are to be fed, the weak and disenfranchised cared for. Indeed, the overarching structure of Jewish agricultural life was orchestrated by Divine law to create a just and holy society. In this light, it makes perfect sense that the evening after we sit with our families and discuss the Passover experience and what it was like to be slaves, we go out to the fields and publicly exhibit that *this* work is holy, and holiness is not relegated exclusively to the Temple but permeates all aspects of our lives.

On the other hand, the Boethusians, who were *kohanim* (priests), were hesitant to "share" the holiness of the Temple. In fact, their theological divergence from the mainstream was far deeper than a Temple-centric view of Judaism, or even the lengths to which they were willing to go to protect the Temple's exclusivity. In an attempt to clarify their philosophy, one of the leading sages of that era, Rabbi Yochanan ben Zakkai, engaged the Boethusians in debate, and questioned their untenable reading of the verses regarding the *omer* offering. One of the elders of the Boethusians gave this explanation: "It is well known that Moshe loved the Jews, and therefore he wished for the Pentecost holiday, which follows the *omer* ceremony by precisely seven weeks, to always fall on a Sunday (which would only be assured if performed on a Saturday night)—thereby creating a 'long weekend.'"[32]

The Boethusians' argument brings several aspects of their philosophy into focus: First, it was convenience, and not holiness, which motivated the Boethusians. They were less interested in the holiness—of the Temple *or* the fields—than in a long weekend. Moreover, we may discern a subtle admission in the subtext of their argument: It was Moshe, and not God, who had devised the commandments. They did not consider the Torah to be Divine; rather, Moshe had "made things up" based on considerations of vacation, travel, convenience—and not holiness.

---

32. Ibid.

In short, these corrupt priests did not truly believe in holiness—not of the fields, not of the Torah's commandments, not even of the Temple in which they served. The rabbis, on the other hand, believed that the holiness of the Temple also existed in the fields. While the Boethusians fought to protect their own turf, the rabbis attempted to enable all of society to feel the holiness of the Temple—even in the fields. This, they taught, was the Will of God: to create a holy society.

Parashat Behar
Living and Loving

As the contours of life and law in Israel's new agricultural society emerge, it becomes clear that the economy outlined by the Torah is designed not only to support farmers and their clientele: Jewish law creates a structure through which even the poor and disenfranchised are provided for and protected.

Throughout this *parashah*, we find a great number of laws that not only mandate feeding the poor, but also laws designed to help those who have fallen on hard times get back on their feet again: farmers who have lost their property and are struggling to reclaim it, as well as others in need of loans or financial support. In these cases, usury is prohibited in a verse that is punctuated by the more general exhortation, "Let your brother live alongside you" (*Vayikra* 25:3).

This verse is understood by the sages of the Talmud as an overarching principle of Jewish ethics, and is applied in various instances of law that may seem far-removed or only tenuously related to the original context in which it is found. Thus, in a talmudic discussion of a highly-fraught moral dilemma, the principle "Let your brother live alongside you" is cited as the rationale for two opposing legal conclusions. The case in question is of two people in the desert; one has enough water to survive, but not enough to insure the survival of his travelling partner. If he shares his water, both travelers will surely die.

A River Flowed from Eden

The Talmud quotes the opinion of a certain all-but anonymous man named Ben Petura (the son of Petura) that it is best to share the water, despite the certain fatal outcome, based on the verse "Let your brother live alongside you." The Talmud then recounts that the great Rabbi Akiva challenged this position on the basis of a different interpretation of this same verse. According to Rabbi Akiva, the verse "Let your brother live alongside you" teaches us that one's own life takes precedence to the life of another.[33]

Prima facia, both of these applications of the verse "Let your brother live alongside you" are strange: If Ben Petura's opinion is followed to its logical conclusion, your brother is not living with you—he is dying with you. On the other hand, if the scenario plays out according to Rabbi Akiva's ruling, your brother is not living with you—he is dying while you live on. Furthermore, we might consider Rabbi Akiva's opinion in light of his most famous ethical pronouncement: "Love your neighbor as yourself; this is the greatest principle of the Torah."[34] Apparently, Rabbi Akiva understood that even loving one's neighbor has limitations, and there are cases in which that love cannot be expressed. Succinctly stated, Rabbi Akiva's reconciliation of these two seemingly opposing principles of Jewish ethics teaches us to love our neighbors as ourselves, but not more than ourselves.

We may gain further insight if we consider that the core and context of the principle "Let your brother live alongside you" is concerned with interest-free money-lending. Specifically, *this* is how your brother lives alongside you—by sharing your resources. However, this sharing of wealth is not intended to reach the point that it endangers your own financial stability. In no way does the verse call for a person to lend money and

33. Talmud Bavli *Bava Metiza* 62a; *Sifra Behar parashah* 5.
34. *Sifra Kedoshim parashah* 2 *perek* 4.

put himself into the position that he himself will be in need of financial assistance. With this in mind, Rabbi Akiva's ruling is more easily understood: Love your neighbor as *yourself*. Insure that your brother can live alongside you, and do not allow him to fall by the wayside—but insure your own well-being in order for this to be possible. Your brother must live alongside you, not instead of you or at the expense of your own life or livelihood. Torah law mandates your own well-being. Self-preservation is the first step in preserving others; if saving someone else endangers your own life, the Torah commands that your brother shall live *with* you.

How did Rabbi Akiva's students understand their teacher's ruling? Did they understand that the case of the two travelers with limited water was an extreme case, and not the norm? Did they understand that only when push comes to proverbial shove, in a zero-sum game situation of life and death, does Rabbi Akiva rule in favor of self-interest over love of one's neighbor? Is it possible that the students of Rabbi Akiva construed their teacher's ethical statement of self-preservation as an endorsement of self-interest at the expense of others? Could it be that Rabbi Akiva's own teaching served as an excuse for his students to act selfishly? Could his own ruling lie at the heart of their lack of respect for one another, each one of them believing that their own status takes precedence over others' dignity?[35]

Even the greatest educator, even the loftiest values, may be misunderstood. Rabbi Akiva could spend a life teaching decency and love, and still have followers misapply his ideas. Rather than using his teachings to create a utopian society, they left death and mourning in their wake. Rather than creating a society based on love, mutual respect, and sharing, they created one based on misanthropy and selfishness.

---

35. See Talmud Bavli *Yevamot* 62b.

The lessons of social justice and mutual responsibility found in *Parashat Behar* are all the more poignant at this time of year, in the *sefirah* period between Pesach and Shavuot. This, the Talmud tells us, is the time of year during which 24,000 students of Rabbi Akiva perished. This was the time of year during which their failure to understand and internalize the Torah's moral imperatives brought about unthinkable loss and destruction. Let us hope that the lessons are not lost on us.

Parashat Bechukotai
You Can Get Satisfaction

Most of *Parashat Bechukotai* deals with the disastrous consequences of rebellion. If the Jewish People fails to obey God's commandments, pain, death and exile will follow. However, this stern warning is prefaced by a description of the utopian existence that awaits us if we fulfill the laws of the Torah. This bright future, and the new society that we are to build, are described in remarkably simple language:

> You will eat your food (bread) to the point of satisfaction, and [you will] live securely in the land. I will grant peace in the land so that you will sleep without fear (Leviticus 26:5-6).

The most prominent feature of this vision of the future is peace, and it has been the hope and prayer of Jews for millennia. The promise that the day would come when they would live as free people in their homeland is a message that empowered and motivated, uplifted and energized not just the individual, but the nation as a whole.

The specific expression of peace, though, speaks to the individual: "You will sleep without fear." The emotional or psychological state it addresses is intimate, almost visceral— the terror in the night which gives no respite. At times, fear is irrational, the product of a psychological pathology; other times, fear is the logical reaction to the realities at hand. Throughout Jewish history, one of the most debilitating aspects of exile was fear itself: The Jew in exile often wandered, but more often feared wandering. Our people often had the collective sense that we were building on quicksand, our fate dependent on the largesse of a fickle despot. As if our lives were subject to the changing winds of an impending storm, the Jewish experience was that of a driven leaf, in constant expectation and dread of being uprooted, of wandering in search of shelter. As the social historian Jacob Katz noted, "It is not a listing of the number of expulsions, whether few or many, which sums up the period, but rather the ever-present dread and possibility of eviction."[36]

The antithesis of this dread is the ability to sleep without fear. It is the certainty, as one puts one's head down at night, that they have reached a place of permanence and security. The blessings which will accrue to us if we follow the commandments demonstrate the fascinating interplay between the political health of a society and the psychological health of the individuals living in that society: The blessings of peace on the national level trickle down to the individual and create tranquility on the most personal, intimate level. This is real peace.

Which leads us to the final element of this utopian vision: satisfaction. This blessing seems so simple, yet its implications are far-reaching. Again, the experience is literally visceral: to be satisfied by our food. To any person who has ever experienced deprivation, this blessing is no trivial matter. For all the world's hungry children—and, for that matter, adults—such a blessing would be literally life altering: "May you never go to sleep hungry. May your food satisfy and satiate you."

---

36. I believe I saw this in Jacob Katz, *Tradition and Crisis*; I am unable to locate the precise citation.

Satisfaction, or the lack thereof, may depend upon two disparate causes, one objective and the other subjective. One cause of dissatisfaction stems from the physical realm of the body's basic needs. If there is simply not enough food to supply the body's energy requirements, it is not satisfied. The other cause lies in the realm of the mind, which is not happy with what it has, despite objective reality.

Western man suffers acutely from this sort of dissatisfaction, despite an unprecedented abundance of goods. Perhaps it is simple jealousy; perhaps someone else has more, perhaps theirs is better, or perhaps we simply want what we do not have. Whatever the cause, modern man's dissatisfaction causes him pain that is often as profound as the pangs of hunger experienced by the child in a drought-stricken third-world country. Psychological pain can be just as debilitating as physical pain, if not even more so; the blessing contained in the verses of *Parashat Bechukotai* addresses both.

Some years ago, I sat down to a meal with a colleague. Before we began to eat, he blessed me, not with the customary *"bon appetite"* or the Hebrew equivalent, *b'te'avon*. Instead, he said, *"la-sovah"*: May your food satisfy you. When I noted this somewhat unusual expression, he explained that this was a blessing he received on a daily basis from his employer, the Chief Rabbi of Israel Rabbi Shlomo Goren, based on the verses of *Parashat Bechukotai*: May you find your food physically and psychologically satisfying.

In addition to the three layers of blessing found in our *parashah*, there is an additional element that should not be overlooked—an element that we mention after every meal: "And you shall eat, and be satiated, and you shall bless God for the land He has given you." In this verse, found in the Book of *Devarim*, we are commanded to go beyond physical satiation, beyond psychological satisfaction, and to consider the spiritual aspects of the food we eat. We must not forget that the source of our sustenance is God.

The Israelites who wandered in the desert for forty years must have had a very unique perspective on this important lesson. Each day they would lift their eyes and watch as their food descended from heaven. This food was perfect in every way—nourishing, satisfying, perfectly suited to their needs, and effortlessly available in unlimited quantities. When they finally entered the Land of Israel and established an agrarian society, they were called upon to retain the absolute certainty they had achieved in the desert, that sustenance comes from God, despite having to work for their daily bread. In their new agricultural society, the Israelites would become partners in their own destiny. They would share responsibility for their sustenance, and effectively become partners with God. This partnership is the source of blessings that they could not experience when they survived on manna—the blessings of *Parashat Bechukotai*. This partnership is the source of true satisfaction, true stability—and true peace.

ספר
במדבר

Parashat B'midbar
An (Un)Necessary Book

As we begin reading the fourth book of the Torah, we cannot help feeling somewhat unsettled. Each of the chapters of *B'midbar* (Numbers) follows in logical sequence; no particular word or sentence causes us unease. Rather, the entire book, as a whole, gives us pause: At face value, this book should never have been written. The events it records should never have happened. The book of *B'midbar* begins as the Israelites leave Mount Sinai, in possession of the precious Torah. Their next stop should have been the Promised Land, their stated destination. Their original itinerary did not include forty years of wandering.

There are two ways of looking at this delay, which is distilled in the name of the book—*B'midbar*, "in the desert" (or perhaps more precisely, "in the wilderness")—reflecting the setting in which the events unfold: Perhaps the people were simply not ready to enter, fight for, capture and rule their own country. They had to come of age, to mature as a nation and to muster the skills and strength they would need before facing the tasks ahead. The desert would be a holding pattern, an incubator. Alternatively, we may find that the desert experience had intrinsic value as an educational experience. To rephrase the question, were the years in the desert a coincidence of geography, or was there a deeper significance to the place in which the Jewish nation came of age? Surely, the Israelites needed a place to collect themselves and to prepare for the conquest of the Land of Israel, and there were few other locales available in which to do so. Nonetheless, there seems to be a greater design behind God's decision to delay their entry into the Land and to extend their sojourn in the desert. Is there something special about the desert that is particularly germane to the process they would undergo?

In the desert, man is exposed, without shelter. Hot days, cold nights, open spaces and no reliable sources of food or water create a situation of unparalleled vulnerability. In this atmosphere, the Israelites' reliance on God was complete, and the certainty that all sustenance comes from God was ingrained upon their collective psyche for all time. This is the quintessential lesson to be learned from the desert, a lesson that could not have been learned as effectively anywhere else.

In this sense, the desert experience is reminiscent of Eden, in which man did no work, yet all his needs were satisfied. While we might not think of the desert as a utopian existence, on a functional level there was something very Eden-like in the Israelites' forty-year sojourn in the desert.

There is another aspect of the desert experience: isolation. Normally, societies are influenced by the ideas, mores and behaviors of other societies—either consciously or subconsciously. Even societies that erect walls—figurative or literal—to resist this inevitable cross-pollination tend to achieve only partial success. The newly freed slaves, at the dawn of their national history and in the early stages of cementing their national identity, may not have been mature enough to withstand negative influences from the pagan societies they would encounter in the Land of Canaan. In this light, it becomes clear why God chose the isolation of the desert for the period of incubation.

This isolation may also be seen as proactive, more positive than a mere avoidance tactic. When Avraham set off to fulfill

God's command and offer up his son Yitzchak, two young men, members of Avraham's household, accompanied them. They reached the appointed place together, but then Avraham divided the group in two: He and Yitzchak would ascend the mountain and serve God, and then rejoin the others. Rabbi Soloveitchik explained this verse as a paradigm of spiritual growth: There comes a time in the life of every seeker of spirituality when he must be alone. However, the verse does not end there: Avraham sees the separation as one stage, and the rejoining of society that follows as no less important a stage in the process.[37]

The Jewish people have a great destiny to fulfill. In order to become a "light unto the nations," we must first be "ignited." This was the essence of the Revelation at Sinai. To cultivate that light and allow it to grow, we needed time; this was the time spent in the desert. Perhaps in a perfect world the former slaves could have entered the Holy Land immediately and had a positive impact on the nations around them; God knew that in reality, they simply were not ready. Just as Avraham needed time alone with Yitzchak, so, too, the Jewish People needed time alone to achieve a full understanding of their relationship with God and His commandments. And just as Avraham descended from that isolated experience of enlightenment and revelation and influenced the entire world, so, too, will his descendants.

---

37. Heard directly from Rabbi Soloveitchik. Compare with *The Rav Speaks*, pp. 43ff.

Parashat Naso
Avoiding Embezzlement

The major thrust of *Parashat Naso* is the initialization of the Temple, particularly the consecration offerings brought by the leaders of each tribe. After an opening section that deals with the stewards of the Temple service, but just before getting into the main topic of discussion, a few seemingly "random" laws are transmitted. The first is a cluster of laws regarding misappropriation of Temple property. The relevance to the main topic of discussion is relatively straightforward: The sparkling new Temple poses new ethical challenges and concerns. Therefore, this is a fitting opportunity for the Torah to teach us that misuse of Temple property, *me'ilah* (literally, "embezzlement"), is a punishable offense.

However, before returning to the main issue at hand— the consecration of the Temple—the Torah transmits three additional laws whose connection to the *parashah*'s main theme seems far more tenuous: The instance of the wife suspected of infidelity (*sotah*), the *nazir*, and the priestly blessings.

The logical flow to the case of *sotah* appears, at first glance, to be based on a linguistic connection: The word *me'ilah*, used to describe embezzlement of Temple resources, is also used to describe the wife's suspected infidelity. In today's world, where the sanctity of marriage is often ignored, the Torah's choice of words gives us pause. By creating this linguistic connection, the Torah creates a parallel between these cases, pointing out with a single word that both embezzlement from the Temple and marital infidelity involve the misuse of something holy. In both cases, a type of sanctity is violated. Infidelity is thus seen not merely as a transgression against a particular spouse; it tramples upon something sacred. This attitude is reflected in the Hebrew word for marriage, *kiddushin*: Marriage is a holy institution. It creates a state of holiness. In such a worldview, an "open marriage" is not an option. The state of holiness, the sanctity of each marriage, is unique and exclusive.

The case of the *sotah* is quite specific in its circumstances: A husband suspects that his wife has had an inappropriate relationship with a particular man, and asks her not to put herself into a compromising situation with that man again. Ignoring his request, the wife secludes herself with the person in question. Clearly, this marriage is dysfunctional. At the very least, the husband is suspicious and jealous, and the wife is insensitive to his concerns and makes poor choices that fuel those suspicions. This deteriorating situation is taken to the Temple, and not to the courts; this is, after all, a question of possible *me'ilah*. Something sacred may well have been violated. Therefore, in a ceremony fraught with symbolism, this very Torah passage— including the Name of God—is destroyed, dissolved in liquid, and ingested by the suspect woman. Apparently, the antidote to the violation of holiness is, literally, a dose of additional holiness. The case is considered so extreme that it calls for destroying the words of the Torah, and the Name of God. This is no trifling matter. The destruction of the sacred text reflects the diminution of holiness that it addresses, for if the sanctity of marriage is brought into question, the sanctity of God's Name suffers as well. An affront to one type of holiness is an affront to both types of holiness.

If, in fact, the woman has been unfaithful, if through her infidelity she shattered something holy, her body will not be capable of ingesting the holy words. If, however, she is innocent, the dose of additional holiness will prove her innocence and carry her to new heights.

In this light, the other seemingly disjointed commandments seem far more germane to the discussion. The *nazir* is a "regular" person who takes upon himself more holiness, voluntarily taking on a quasi-*kohen* status. In allowing this self-deprivation and self-definition, the Torah recognizes that even in the world of the mundane, individuals may occasionally feel the need to elevate their own personal level of holiness. The passage that immediately follows that of the *nazir* is the text of the priestly blessing, *birkat kohanim*, the conduit through which holiness is transmitted to the masses.

The Temple is the epicenter of holiness in the world. However, Judaism is designed to bring holiness into our everyday lives. Holiness is not the exclusive property of the Temple or of the *kohanim* who serve in the Temple. The challenge is to bring holiness into our marriages, our homes, our lives. We are required to conduct ourselves, and our business and personal relationships, with a constant eye toward holiness. When holiness is ignored or, even worse, banished from our personal lives, the individual must undergo a spiritual adjustment, represented by the *nazir* state. On the national level, the *kohanim* play a dual role: They serve as representatives of the people in the Temple service, but at the same time they transmit the holiness of the Temple and spread it throughout the land, by teaching Torah and also by allowing the holy blessings to flow through their fingers to touch the lives of each and every member of society.

Parashat BeHaalotcha
Despair and Hope

At one time or another, anyone may feel overwhelmed, either due to work-related stress, conflict with co-workers, friends, one's spouse or children—or a combination of factors. For some people, problems have a way of metastasizing, spreading noxious despair that overtakes the more positive aspects of life. The pressures seem too much to handle; the problems seem insurmountable. At such times, we need to prioritize, to break down the tasks into manageable units and view them as individual challenges, in order to keep despair from overwhelming us.

Sometimes, we suffer from feelings of inadequacy because we operate under the illusion that other people have perfect lives. Just as our neighbor's lawn seems neat and trimmed and perfectly green, we think other peoples' entire lives are "greener"—more perfect, more well-adjusted. This misperception may be even more acute in terms of our spiritual heroes, whom we believe to be perfect in every way. The challenges experienced by the average person seem foreign to these great souls—at least in the hagiographic accounts of their lives.

Perhaps this is why the words of desperation and despair uttered by Moshe, our teacher and leader *par excellence*, the greatest of our prophets, come as such a shock: "I cannot be responsible for this entire nation! It's too hard for me! If You are going to do this to me, just do me a favor and kill me"

(*B'midbar* 11:14-15). Perhaps this is just a turn of phrase, similar to the popular retort, "Just shoot me." However, just as one should not make such a flippant comment to a person holding a gun, it may have been less than prudent for Moshe to say those words to God, who is perfectly and absolutely capable of fulfilling his request.

It seems that Moshe had reached his breaking point. In context, his despair is understandable: Moshe had just invited his father-in-law Hovav to join the Israelites' epic march to the Promised Land. After more than a year encamped at Sinai, the time had come to make their way to the Land of Israel. Moshe speaks in the present tense: "We are going to the Land that God has promised us." His excitement is palpable. We can almost hear the breathlessness of his anticipation as his great dream is about to come true. Unfortunately, he did not know what we, the readers, do: The bitter reality is that Moshe will not complete the triumphant march that is about to begin. He will not achieve the final goal; he will never enter the Land of Israel. And herein lies the rub: Profound disappointment is born of extreme expectations.[38]

We may liken this to the disappointment experienced by a young person who goes on a seemingly successful first date, but does not get a call for a second date. However disheartening this may be, this disappointment cannot be compared to that of a bride or groom who has set a date for the wedding, reserved the hall, ordered the dress or stood for the final suit fitting—when the call comes that the wedding is off. Extreme excitement and anticipation transforms into devastating darkness. This is what Moshe experienced: He speaks in the present tense. He believes that all obstacles have been overcome, and the next stop is the Promised Land. And now, without warning, a litany of complaints causes him to understand that his dreams

---

38. Rabbi Soloveitchik made this point in a lecture delivered 6/7/77.

will be frustrated. Perhaps, as my late teacher Rabbi Yosef Soloveitchik suggested, Moshe had a premonition; perhaps it was something more concrete. Whatever the reasons that caused it, Moshe experienced the crushing fall from the height of his expectations—plummeting from "We are going," we are on our way to fulfilling our destiny—to the disheartening reality that he faced. The march to the Land of Israel that ignited his spirit and filled him with joy was a trip Moshe would not complete. The three-day journey would take years, and he would not live to see it completed.

Depression comes when dreams disintegrate, degenerating into a debilitating nightmare.

Moshe's plea is an expression of despair. He knows deep inside that he will fail, and this sudden realization is crippling. Why should he carry on? Why continue the charade of leadership if he will not complete his task? Nonetheless, God stands by his side. Rather than accepting Moshe's pleas and "putting him out of his misery," God responds: If you cannot do this alone, I will provide you with help.

Perhaps this is a lesson for us all. When we feel overwhelmed, when we want to say, "Just shoot me," free me from this burden, release me from responsibilities I am incapable of living up to, our prayer should be, "God, please give me strength. Please send me help, and please stand by me. Together, we will accomplish what You placed me on earth to achieve."

Parashat Sh'lach
Have I Got a Land for You!

The tragic tale of the spies is well known: Moshe handpicks leaders to pay a visit to the Promised Land, but the mission spirals out of control. Upon hearing the spies' report, mass hysteria breaks out, and, as a result, a death sentence is handed down to all those involved: The entire generation that had been liberated from Egypt would perish in the desert.

What happened? How did such a failure of leadership come about? And how were these erstwhile leaders capable of leading the people so far astray?

My revered teacher, Rabbi Yosef Dov Soloveitchik, made an observation that is the key to understanding the entire episode: The sin committed by the spies was, quite simply, that they saw themselves as spies.[39] Moshe had not tasked them with spying— not on the land, not on its inhabitants. He instructed them to visit the land, to tour it and let it make an impression on them. The "spies" sinned because they behaved like spies: They misconstrued their mandate, and grossly over-estimated their own expertise and importance.

And yet, we may ask, if they were not meant to act as spies, what was the purpose of their visit?

Their mission is best understood with the help of an analogy: When a matchmaker approaches a young man or woman, the matchmaker describes the attributes of the intended. If the

---

39. In a lecture delivered 6/4/75.

match sounds promising, both sides agree to meet, but they will go to the date with a critical eye. Does their date match up to the matchmaker's glowing description? Do they find the other person attractive? Intelligent? Appropriate? Can they imagine spending the rest of their life with this person? Can they love this person? Is there chemistry? Is there any attraction that brings them together and increases the odds that this relationship will endure and grow?

In a very real sense, this is how the spies approached their mission. Their initial report was that they found the land attractive; only later did they add the caveat that, attraction notwithstanding, the land was unobtainable, "out of their league." When Calev (Caleb) challenged them, insisting that the land was within their reach, they began to denigrate the land itself, perhaps in an attempt to justify their feelings of inadequacy, describing it as "a land that devours its inhabitants."

However, to return to our analogy, let us consider what a first date would be like if the matchmaker was God. What if God Himself said to a young man or woman, "Long ago I created a soul. This soul was subsequently divided into two. Half the soul was placed in your body; the other half of this soul resides in the body of the person I would like you to meet. I would like to introduce you to your soul-mate."

It would be safe to assume that the young man or woman in such a scenario would agree to go on the date, but their purpose would be different. They would probably spend little or no time or effort on superficial, inconsequential issues: Tall or short, fat or thin—these make no difference at all. This first date would be far less of an exercise in critical judgment, and far more of an opportunity to start the next chapter of their life together. The purpose of this date is to reunite.

This was the purpose of the mission with which Moshe entrusted the emissaries. A careful reading of their mandate, of the questions he asked them to consider during their visit, makes this clear. Moshe did not ask them to pass judgment or plot the course of the impending conquest. He posed rhetorical questions aimed at helping the emissaries appreciate the beauty of the Promised Land. Rather than reading Moshe's question as an earnest, worried, "Is it, or is it not, a good land," we should read Moshe's question as, "Is this a good land, or what!" The last words Moshe spoke to the emissaries illustrate the point:

> What is this land? Is it rich or lean? Does it have trees?
> Be strong, and bring fruit from the land (*B'midbar* 13:20).

There seems to be a phrase missing. We would expect Moshe to have said, "Does it have trees? If so, bring back a sample of the fruit of the land." However, Moshe knows there is fruit; this is a land flowing with milk and honey. More importantly, this is the land that God promised to Avraham, Yitzchak, and Yaakov. This is the Promised Land. This is the land in which the Jewish People would realize their dreams, fulfill their destiny. Could it be anything less than what God Himself had described?

The sin of the spies was their belief that they were, in fact, spies. Being important leaders, they assumed that their critical opinion was significant, and they felt it was their duty to be critical. They went on their mission to catch the matchmaker "red-handed" in an exaggeration or even an outright lie.

Moshe envisioned their first date with the Promised Land quite differently. He sent emissaries whom he thought would have a finely developed sense of history and destiny. He assumed that they knew and understood that the Land of Israel and the Jewish People are soul-mates, made for one another, created as one and separated, only to be reunited, destined to fall in love and live together happily ever after.

Parashat Korach
Living the Dream, Ignoring Reality

Opportunism, demagoguery, manipulation, jealousy, conniving, self-destruction: These are just some of the words that come to mind when considering Korach and his rebellion.

Moshe's leadership was challenged many times, both before and after the Exodus from Egypt. Usually, these attacks arose in times of crisis; scarcity of resources has a way of bringing out the worst in people. Whether it was a shortage of straw for making bricks in Egypt, bread or water in the desert, or meat instead of manna, each time the people felt vulnerable they lashed out at God and Moshe for the "foolhardy" plan of taking a nation of "content" slaves into the treacherous, unforgiving desert.

The crisis that immediately preceded Korach's rebellion, the sin of the spies, differed in both texture and result. Convinced by the spies that conquest of the Land of Israel was beyond their capabilities, the people panicked. They were terrified that they would soon be utterly decimated on the battlefield, and vented their desperation by verbally attacking God, and physically threatening Moshe and Aharon. Their punishment was meted out swiftly: The leaders who had fomented the panic died immediately, and the followers—those who allowed themselves to disregard the miraculous nature of their sustenance and guidance in the desert, those who abandoned their faith in God and His most faithful servant—received a death sentence.

144

A River Flowed from Eden

The punishment for the sin of the spies caused a tectonic shift: For the entire generation of adults who had marched out of Egypt and received the Torah at Sinai, the Promised Land would remain an unfulfilled promise. A new type of despair hovered over the camp, and, for a certain type of twisted mind, the time seemed ripe for challenging Moshe's leadership. Logically, the preceding chapters should have made it abundantly clear that Moshe was *the* leader: Divinely appointed, and unparalleled in his relationship with God and the protection he enjoyed because of that relationship. Any rational person, no matter how jealous of Moshe's status, should have seen that attacking Moshe would be foolhardy and futile. And yet, people often behave illogically. Human beings have the capacity, even the tendency, to ignore what is best for themselves and their families, and instead opt to be captivated by fantasies. Pleasant daydreams are often more compelling than stark reality.

Korach suffered from delusions of grandeur. He saw himself, and not Moshe, as the one deserving the adulation of the crowds. Under the sway of his own visions of self-importance and over-estimation of his own capabilities, he interpreted the events recounted in the previous chapters as indications of Moshe's failure as a leader, and he seized the opportunity presented by the despair that had made inroads into the camp. To be sure, Korach was talented. His oratorical skills were obvious, particularly his ability to rally the crowd behind a wonderful, compelling slogan: "All the people are holy." His following grew with each new sound bite. He appealed to the disgruntled and disenfranchised, and created a confederacy of malcontents to launch a challenge against Moshe's leadership.

There was, however, a path not taken—a path that would have led to glory instead of infamy. No matter what problems, real or imagined, Korach perceived in the camp, rather than exploiting these problems to catapult himself to leadership,

Parashat Korach

Korach could have taken the path chosen by Yitro. When Moshe's father-in-law Yitro arrived at the Israelites' encampment, he immediately identified what he saw as a very serious problem: Every question, every dispute, big or small, landed at the door of Moshe's tent. Yitro, who was a successful religious leader in his own right, advised Moshe to delegate authority in order to release the bottleneck that threatened to frustrate the people and exhaust Moshe's personal capabilities. Yitro did not attempt to exploit the situation for his own purposes, nor was his advice offered in order to feed his own ego. He offered constructive criticism and practical suggestions, and Moshe accepted Yitro's advice in the spirit in which it was offered, implementing Yitro's plan to lead the people more effectively and efficiently. Perhaps this is the reason that one of the most famous portions of the Torah is named for Yitro, and he is remembered until this day in a positive light.

Korach, on the other hand, used his considerable talents to attack and weaken Moshe. He, like Yitro, was related to Moshe; Korach was Moshe's cousin. But rather than offering a helping hand, he waged an attack. Instead of support, Korach offered slogans; instead of taking a hard look at reality, Korach embraced his own beautiful daydream of status, adulation, power—a pipe dream that ended in his own death and the deaths of those whom he manipulated and led astray.

Korach, like Yitro, is immortalized in a *parashah* that bears his name, but the story this *parashah* tells is a cautionary tale of an opportunistic demagogue who manipulates his unsuspecting followers with conniving and ultimately self-destructive words. We can only imagine what a positive impact he could have had on the Jewish People had he chosen the other path, using his strength to build and bolster Moshe's leadership and create a better reality for his people, rather than chasing his own destructive fantasies.

Parashat Chukat
Embracing Torah

Death permeates this *parashah*. There are the obvious deaths—
Moshe's older siblings, Miriam and Aharon—and the not-
so-obvious deaths: At some point, very quietly, the Torah has
"fast forwarded" and skipped 38 years between the previous
parashah, *Korach*, and this *parashah*, *Chukat*. All the adults that
left Egypt, the generation that had been condemned to death
as a result of the sin of the spies, has perished. Moshe himself
receives a death sentence; the new generation will enter the
Promised Land without him.

Parashat Chukat is comprised not only of narrative that is
rife with overtones of death, but also of laws that are concerned
with the same subject. The *parashah* begins by introducing the
laws of the red heifer ritual, used as an antidote to the impurity
that results from contact with the dead.

This is by no means our first encounter with death in the
Torah. From time immemorial, from the dawn of human
experience, from the beginning of the Torah, people have been
dying. On the level of biological reality, we understand death;
it results either from sudden trauma which compromises the
integrity of the biological system, or from systemic breakdown
caused by years of wear and tear. But if the mechanics of death
are part and parcel of life, it is the philosophical aspect of death
that haunts and torments us, and it is regarding this aspect of
death that the Torah's philosophy is remarkable.

Parashat Chukat

In *Parashat Chukat* and elsewhere, we cannot escape the conclusion that death is not a necessary element of the human condition. The physical realities of death which we consider immutable facts of life need not be so; death as we know it was only one of the possible options for human existence, and it was the option chosen by man himself. Death became a part of our lives in the Garden of Eden, as a result of partaking from the Tree of Knowledge of Good and Evil. Moreover, even in Eden, even after the sin, there was still another tree that was the antithesis of, or the antidote to death: the Tree of Life. There are, then, two antidotes to death: the red heifer ritual, which removes the spiritual stain left behind by death, and the Tree of Life, which completely eradicates death.

Taken together, these two antidotes teach us that although on a biological level death seems inevitable, on a theological level, death need never have been a part of our existence. Had man refrained, as commanded, from eating the fruit of the Tree of Knowledge of Good and Evil, or, even after eating from it, had man eaten from the Tree if Life as well, death would have remained only a philosophical possibility.

What are these miraculous antidotes? What is the un-fathomable secret that would make death external to human reality? What is this source of eternal life? It is Torah, the common denominator between the Tree of Life and the red heifer ritual. Both are identified as "Torah," not in a general sense but in a very specific sense. In the book of Proverbs (3:18), the Torah is described as a "Tree of Life to those who embrace it," while in our present *parashah*, the red heifer ritual is introduced as "*the* decree of Torah" (*zot chukat ha-Torah*)—in a definitive, exclusive sense. Torah is as accessible as the fruit of a tree, and as mysterious as the most inscrutable Divine decree; it is both attainable yet of unfathomable, unlimited depth. Torah is the very source of eternal life. God Himself gave this gift to mankind at the dawn of creation, in the form of the Tree of Life—but man forfeited the rights to it. Later, in an almost unbelievable act of kindness, God gave mankind a second chance: At Sinai, God once again gave man access to this source of eternal life, in the form of Torah. Equally unbelievably, mankind once again failed to seize the opportunity.

Had things worked out differently at Sinai, had the Torah been properly received, death would have been vanquished. The first steps in this process were experienced at the foot of Mount Sinai: Tradition tells us that in preparation for receiving the Torah, all the sick were healed, all the infirm were restored to full health.[40] Even today, so many hospitals are named in commemoration of the great healing experienced at Mount Sinai. Had the people only stayed the course, had they not squandered the opportunity to take hold of the source of eternal life that is Torah, there would never have been a need for hospitals at all; sickness and death would have become memories, theoretical possibilities that belonged to the abandoned path of ignorance and impurity. Instead, when Moshe descended with the Tablets of Testimony, the people were busy singing and dancing in worship of a calf made of gold. We would do well to imagine how history would have played out had they instead danced and celebrated around Moshe as he descended from on high, grasping the Torah he had received from God's hand.

By choosing the calf over Torah and turning their backs on Moshe, who was the ultimate symbol of God's transmission of Torah to mankind, they once again chose death over life.

As a result of their choice, they should have been eradicated on the spot; if not for Moshe's intercession, that is precisely what would have happened. Instead, their sin re-mapped the course of history, and continues to resonate in this *parashah*.

---

40. Rashi, *Shemot* 19:11.

According to a tradition cited by Rashi, the golden calf served as the impetus for the red heifer ritual: As a counterbalance to death, to the choice they made that was symbolized by a calf, they would be commanded to sacrifice this very special cow, a heifer of unique color; the mother cow would be used to "clean up" the mess created by the mischievous calf. The rebellion of the golden calf is thus transformed into a Torah experience, symbolized by the red heifer and all its mystery. The desire to create and worship a concrete god is combatted with an act of surrender to a law we do not understand, and the horror of the physical reality of death is tempered by the Torah's reminder, through the red heifer ritual, that this condition is not inevitable. Just as death is the result of our own poor choices, so, too, can eternal life be achieved by grasping the Tree of Life—Torah.

Tragically, the people's poor choices did not end at Mount Sinai. They continued to reject the source of life. Over and over, they failed to embrace Moshe, failed to take advantage of the opportunity to dance around him and rejoice in the man who was, for all time, the embodiment of Torah. Their litany of complaints seems unending: In *Parashat Chukat*, they are incapable of finding an appropriate way to address the water crisis, and revert to their habitual complaining, nagging, baiting and loss of faith. In responding to them, Moshe deviates ever so slightly from God's instructions, and momentarily ceases to embody Torah. For this, he forfeits the right to lead the people into the Land of Israel and the privilege of serving as the Messiah. Had Moshe led the people into the Land of Israel, ushering in the messianic age, death would have been eradicated and history would have reached its apex.

Sadly, the people never properly embraced Moshe. They continued to turn away from the Tree of Life and Moshe, our Torah Master. Death remained an inextricable part of their lives, and Moshe, the living antidote to death, perished along with them. But unlike them, when Moshe died, no one became impure; God Himself conducted the funeral and burial. Moshe had no part in the sin of the golden calf, and no ashes of the red heifer were needed after his passing.

All of us, descendants of those who failed time and time again to choose life, continue to grapple with death. For our ancestors, the ashes of the red heifer served as a reminder of what might have been had they made better choices. Sadly, after generations of similarly poor choices, even this spiritual antidote is no longer available to us. Instead, we live with death and impurity, facing the consequences of the choices we continue to make.

Parashat Balak
Reading Anti-Semites

Parashat Balak begins with a peek into a world that both attracts and repulses us: It is a conversation among anti-Semites regarding the Jewish Problem. This conversation interests us because, on some level, we want to know what others are saying about our people—even to the point of obsession that enthralls and overwhelms our own self-awareness. On the other hand, we find the stereotypes and animus abhorrent. Anyone who has ever overheard or participated in a conversation regarding the Jews in which the interlocutors are unaware that one of the participants is Jewish, has experienced this strange feeling.

The perceptions of those who hate us are encapsulated in a beautiful but painful joke, which has certainly known many renditions and incarnations. The following is a version set in Nazi Germany:

> *Rabbi Altmann and his secretary were sitting in a coffeehouse in Berlin in 1935. "Herr Altmann," said his secretary, "I notice you're reading Der Stürmer! I can't understand why. A Nazi libel sheet! Are you some kind of masochist, or, God forbid, a self-hating Jew?"*

> *"On the contrary, Frau Epstein. When I used to read the Jewish papers, all I learned about were pogroms, riots in Palestine, and assimilation in America. But now that I*

read Der Stürmer, I see so much more: The Jews control all the banks, we dominate in the arts, and we're on the verge of taking over the entire world. You know—it makes me feel a whole lot better!"

This basic idea is not only true, but as old as the Book of *B'midbar*. *Parashat Balak* begins with a description of the overall climate of those times:

> The Moavites became petrified because the [Israelite] People were so numerous. They were disgusted by the Israelites (*B'midbar* 22:3).

Here are two common elements: There are "so many" Jews, and they are "disgusting." The Moavites' description of the Jews is telling:

> Moav said to the elders of Midian, "Now the [Israelite] community will lick up everything around us, just as a bull licks up all the vegetation in the field" (ibid.).

The first step is, and always has been, the dehumanization of the Jews; they are compared to animals. But the second step is the particular choice of metaphor. In this case, they are likened to a powerful, destructive animal—a bull. This description is even more striking when we recall that earlier in the Book of *B'midbar*, when the scouts returned from their mission to explore the Promised Land, they made a fascinating comment:

> While we were there, we saw the titans. They were sons of the giants, descendants of titans. We felt in our own eyes like tiny grasshoppers. And so we were in their eyes (*B'midbar* 13:33).

It is perfectly legitimate to describe one's adversary through the use of images or allegory, especially when the adversary seems particularly unusual or powerful. Similarly, it is perfectly acceptable to describe your own feelings—what it felt like to be in the proximity of this adversary. What is not legitimate is to project your own perception onto others, to decide how your adversary perceives you. The spies contended that they knew how the residents of the land saw them: "We were like grasshoppers in their eyes." Conversely, Moav saw the Jews not as grasshoppers, but as a powerful bull that swallows up the field.

Here, then, is the difference between the assessment of current events found in Jewish newspapers, as opposed to that found in the news outlets of our enemies: We project our own weakness onto their perception, while they see our power.

A second element can be discerned from Bil'am's famous words:

How good are your tents Yaakov, the dwelling places of Israel! (*B'midbar* 24:5)

Bil'am sees a large camp that is unified. The commentaries on this verse explain that when Bil'am saw the layout of the camp, he saw something remarkable: The doors and windows of the tents did not face one another. He saw that the Israelites had achieved unity, but not at the price of enforced uniformity. He saw a large nation that worked toward achieving its goals as one body politic, yet each individual within the camp retained their right to privacy, personal autonomy and dignity. Even more remarkable is the fact that this is the camp of the Jews. The Torah does not whitewash or omit the many internecine struggles, revolts, and transgressions that this camp had already survived. And yet, despite all of our perceived differences, the outsider sees us as a unified nation living in harmony and moving forward in solidarity.

Today, our own newspapers are full of the language of disunity and despair: conflict between different segments of our own nation based on differences that are so minute as to be imperceptible to outside observers. Even worse, like the spies in the desert, we continue to project our own insecurities onto others, and fail to see our greatness. We assume that we know how others see us, and fail to see ourselves as we truly are—or as others see us.

Sometimes the best medicine for the Jews is to see the newspapers of those who hate us. It is there that we can read about our power as it is perceived by others. It is there that we can be bolstered by the unity others ascribe to us. At the very least, by reading those newspapers, we will be reminded that we face common threats, and that the best way to fight these threats is to look past our own small differences, and to utilize our power—the power we often forget we possess.

Parashat Pinchas
Fanaticism

Pinchas was a fanatic. As anyone raised in Western society will tell you, fanatics are bad, and the only thing worse than a fanatic is a religious fanatic. We have been raised on the axiomatic, nearly-religious certainty that religious fanaticism is the root of all evil, the underlying cause of every conflict around the globe. And yet, the biblical account of Pinchas' response to Zimri and Kozbi sends us some confusing messages.

Zimri and Kozbi, each a member of their respective society's elite, make a very public display of their defiance of religious and social dictates. In response, in what may be called the archetypical act of religious fanaticism, Pinchas appears to take the law into his own hands: He commits a double murder, yet he is rewarded with eternal priesthood as well as the "covenant of peace." If ever there was an ironic award, this is it—or so it would seem.

Zimri and Kozbi do not seem all that strange to us. We, too, live in a time and place in which boundaries are constantly re-examined, redefined, and often discarded publicly, demonstratively. Religion is under siege, in retreat. Popular culture exhorts us to "imagine... no religion"—such a time, we are assured, will be utopian. Without religion there will be no more war; peace will break out all over.

This axiom, we are assured, is self-evident, despite the abundance of evidence to the contrary, namely, the entire

156

"body of work" of the 20th Century, in which more people were killed than in any previous century—perhaps more than throughout all of history combined (some have put the number at 262 million victims). Yet most of these lives were not taken in the name of religion: Socialism, communism and National Socialism (also known as Nazism), the most infamous among recent history's murderous movements, all had strong roots in atheism and paganism and were, for the most part, ideologically opposed to religion. Nonetheless, we tend not to let the facts interfere with our preconceived notion that it is religion that creates strife and is the real *casus belli*. Modern thinkers tend to simply disregard other "minor" factors that continue to bring out the worst in people and nations, such as greed, jealousy, and tribalism.

Looking at the bigger picture, we may say that what lies at the dark heart of war is the human desire to control others—economically, politically, socially, and sexually.

This is where religion can be the solution and not the problem: Religion creates boundaries. Religion makes value judgments. Right and wrong have objective meaning. Religion not only makes these judgments, but expects that mankind live up to these values. Both compliance and sin are significant and conscious choices. Judaism is predicated on the optimistic view of human nature, that man has the greatness to practice self-control; without this expectation, Judaism would be an absurdity. Judaism reminds us that humankind is created in the image of God, and has the capacity for godliness, for greatness. Although man certainly has the capacity to be victorious in the struggle to dominate others, Judaism teaches that true victory is in the battle with one's own ego, and true greatness is achieved when one conquers the desire to control others.

The self-restraint that lies at the core of Jewish values is what Bil'am saw as he observed the Israelite camp from afar.

He saw boundaries, and the respect for privacy that is the basis of community. He saw religious and social demarcations that serve as the basis for unity. Instinctively, he understood that a People with such self-control could not be cursed. Their essential character was deserving of blessing, and was a source of blessing for others.

Zimri and Kozbi, on the other hand, left little room for misinterpretation. Theirs was an act calculated to break the religious, cultural, moral, social and personal boundaries that keep the nation together. Pinchas understood the threat they posed, foresaw the devolution of society that would result from the deconstruction of Jewish mores. He knew how a world without boundaries would look: like an endless battlefield for individual power.

Pinchas's actions should be read in context: A plague was sweeping through the camp. God's wrath had been kindled because of the idolatry and adultery that had spread through the camp, both of which were related to the worship of Ba'al Peor. Apparently, adherents of this type of idolatry believed that all things natural are holy; therefore, sexuality was part and parcel of their cultic practice.

God commands Moshe to have the worshippers of Ba'al put to death. Moshe turns to the tribal leaders, the judges, to implement God's command, to kill the perpetrators and thereby halt the deadly plague. Zimri, a leader of the tribe of Shimon, chooses to side with the sinners: Disregarding God's specific instructions to kill the perpetrators, Zimri makes a public statement, behaving obscenely in the most public, sanctified forum, and joins the idolatrous, adulterous mob. Only then does Pinchas step forward and kill Zimri and the woman with whom he so publicly flaunted the word of God, the leadership of Moshe, the sanctity of the Tabernacle, the purity of the Jewish camp and the Jewish home, as well as the most basic tenet of Judaism, monotheism.

Pinchas was not a vigilante; he acted to fulfill God's explicit instructions, and did, in fact, stop the plague that had already claimed so many lives. Pinchas was, indeed, a fanatic; he was fanatically dedicated to peace. For his fanatical defense of the boundaries with which peace is maintained, God rewarded him with what he most desired: He gave him a covenant of peace:

> Pinchas, the son of Elazar and grandson of Aharon the *Kohen*, was the one who zealously took up My cause among the Israelites and turned My anger away from them, so that I did not destroy them in My demand for exclusive worship. Therefore, tell him that I have given him My covenant of peace. This shall imply a covenant of eternal priesthood to him and his descendants after him. It is [given to him] because he zealously took up God's cause and made atonement for the Israelites (*B'midbar* 25:12).

Pinchas is also no stranger to us: Like him, we are often faced with the challenge posed by moral relativism that threatens to tear down the boundaries and dilute the values upon which our lives are predicated. Like Pinchas, we, too, often must fight in order to achieve peace. However, such battles must be waged only with Divine instruction and purity of spirit. Too many who think they have license to kill, who see themselves as modern-day incarnations of Pinchas, take the law into their own hands. They do not achieve peace; their actions serve only to further weaken the boundaries that keep the community whole.

May God bless us with the wisdom, vision, and strength of Pinchas, and bring to fruition the Priestly Blessing of peace.

Parashat Matot
"Shall Your Brothers Go To War While You Sit Here?"

"Shall your brothers go to war while you sit here?" With these words Moshe hurls a devastating moral attack against the tribes of Reuven (Reuben) and Gad, an attack that reverberates until this very day, and is used as ammunition against those who live in the modern State of Israel yet choose to take advantage of the deferments from military service available to Torah scholars.

As the Jews drew nearer to the Promised Land, they came into possession of lush grazing land, and two tribes expressed a desire to make their homestead east of Israel. In short, they sought to trade their future portion in the land of their forefathers for the green pastures across the border. For them, the Promised Land would remain an unfulfilled promise—not because God did not want to keep His promise, but because they were less interested in what the Land of Israel had to offer than they were in the lucrative opportunity they saw on the outside.

Their request was met with a rhetorical question, a response so full of moral outrage that its critical tone was unmistakable: "Shall your brothers go to war while you sit here?" The historic moment in time should not be overlooked: The conquest of the Land of Israel and the very existence of a Jewish national entity in the Land of the Patriarchs hung in the balance.

Upon closer inspection, their wish not to be a part of the "Zionist" enterprise is not really analogous to those who live in Israel today and choose not to fight. We have become so accustomed to hearing these words used out of context that we fail to take note of the differences: Those who live in Israel, regardless of their political orientation or the degree to which they take part in national or military institutions, do not fit squarely into the moral attack hurled by Moshe against the two tribes who sought to remain outside the Land. When considered in context, Moshe's charge against those who would choose the lush fields over the Land of Israel would be more appropriately directed at modern-era Jews who choose to remain in the diaspora rather than taking part in the rebuilding of the Jewish Homeland.

Moshe's response to the two tribes' request goes one step further, lending context and depth to his critique:

> And why do you discourage the heart of the people of Israel from going over to the land which God has given them? This is what your fathers did, when I sent them from Kadesh-Barnea to see the land (*B'midbar* 32:7-8).

Moshe compares their request to the sin of the spies, perhaps the most nefarious episode endured during his tenure. He identifies the crux of the spies' perfidy not simply in the rejection of the Land of Israel, but in the fear they instilled in the hearts of the people. This fear escalated into panic and led to a massive breakdown of faith and purpose. The spies' insidious report caused the nation to doubt their leaders, to lose sight of their goals. The entire community of Israel began to have second thoughts about the Land and their collective destiny. A similar charge cannot be made against those who live in Israel today, even if they do not share the burden of protecting the Land and the People of Israel.

The moral imperative Moshe conveyed in his response to the breakaway tribes can have practical implications and applications today: First, for those living in Israel who do not serve: By any moral and religious logic, those who live in Israel must offer their full support to our soldiers and their sacred mission. Too often, demagogues get caught up in their self-serving ideology and attack the State, the government, and the I.D.F. as if they are all part of an elaborate plot designed to uproot Jewish values. The role of the army is far more prosaic; if they are involved in a plot of any kind, it is a plot to protect the lives and freedoms of as many Jews as possible. This is a responsibility that must be shared by each and every one of us.

Too often, the discussion regarding military service dredges up old arguments and grudges, and present-day reality is ignored. Rather than focusing on internal battles of the past, rabbinic authorities should treat themselves to a healthy dose of reality. The same rabbis who attack the army and proscribe military service often hand down halakhic rulings that permit soldiers to break Shabbat laws when lives are in danger. It is a strange sort of cognitive dissonance that allows them to understand that our soldiers' efforts are sacred acts, while at the same time labeling those who perform this life-saving labor as impure. Is a soldier who risks his own life for the protection of his brethren no more than a "shabbos goy"? In point of fact, today's I.D.F. may have more religiously observant officers than secular ones. The iconic "kibbutznik warrior" of the past has been eclipsed by the brave *kippah*-clad graduate of a religious-Zionist yeshiva.

Among the rabbis who saw things differently, two come to mind: One was my revered teacher, Rabbi Yisrael Gustman, who, upon seeing the graves in the military cemetery on Mount Herzl, declared, *"Kulam kedoshim,"* "They are all holy martyrs." Another is Rabbi Shlomo Zalman Auerbach. When a student asked the Rabbi's permission to take a short leave from the yeshiva in Jerusalem to travel to pray at the "graves of the righteous," Rabbi Auerbach told him that he need go no further than Mount Herzl, to the military cemetery.

These great rabbis recognized that our brothers who went to war and did not return were holy. It behooves all those who remain in yeshiva and devote themselves to learning Torah, to bolster the spirit of those around them and aid in the national effort in any way they can. First and foremost, they must recognize the sanctity of the sacrifice others are making on their behalf, and the holiness of those who have fought, and continue to fight, to secure the freedom to build and populate great centers of Torah learning in Israel—especially those who paid for these blessings with their lives.

As for those who have chosen the diaspora as home: Make sure that your choices do not instill fear in the hearts of those who dwell in Zion. Be active in your support: Send your children to Israel. Allow them to serve in the army if they express the desire to do so. Remember that this moral fortitude and bravery is the culmination of a proper education. Consider the Israelis who give three years of their lives to military service, and then continue to disrupt their normal routine for a month or more each year for decades thereafter. Keeping that time-frame in mind, create a parallel structure for donating resources or time to Jewish causes, and strengthen the spirit of those who live in Israel. Israel should be more than just a destination for vacations. It is the inheritance of all Jews, and a part of our personal and collective destiny.

Parashat Mas'ei
Walking in Circles

There is something that may seem rather depressing about the start of the final *parashah* in the book of *B'midbar*: The *parashah* begins with a retrospective of the various stops comprising the Israelites' forty-year ordeal in the desert. Knowing, as we do, that the original plan had been to leave Egypt, make a quick stop at Sinai, and commence the glorious march to Israel, the stark contrast with the reality of their long sojourn, punctuated by death and despair, is tragic. It is clear to us, as it must have been to them, that for the most part, they were not really going anywhere. They were, in a sense, walking in circles; the main objective was avoiding their desired destination.

Generally, we view the world in a linear fashion: There is a clearly defined beginning, and a clear end. We have objectives, and we expend time and energy approaching our goals along a linear axis, with the objective serving as the terminal point. This is the way most of us see our lives; we gauge success by the progress made along the path that leads to the fulfillment of our objectives.

While Judaism does not reject this linear view of the world, it does have many cyclical elements as well. Our calendar marks the passing of days and years, and although each day is different and precious, every seventh day we return to the holy Sabbath. Likewise, we celebrate the appearance of the new moon, marking new months and holidays which return, like old friends or cherished family members, each year. The cyclical nature of the calendar makes many of the significant aspects of our lives more of a circle than a straight line.

The Jews traveling in the wilderness were not simply trying to get from the land of Egypt to the Promised Land. Had that been the goal, we may safely say that the forty-year sojourn was a failure: A distance that could have been traversed in days took years. However, the desert experience went beyond the linear, goal-oriented view of history, and it incorporated the circular, cyclical approach in a very significant way.

The goal-oriented, linear mindset governs our daily life as we rush from place to place, even though we are capable of altering our own perceptions of time and progress: A small delay in the daily commute is enough to thoroughly shake us up, but our experience of the same travel time when we are on vacation is completely different. Our perceptions become completely altered by the smallest change in our linear approach to time.

This was made clear to me some years ago, when my wife and I travelled to South Africa. While the main purpose of the trip was to teach, we were able to take some time to see the sights. Cape Town is one of the most beautiful cities in the world, and its citizens took great pride in showing us around. Many things caught our eye, and I was particularly taken with one tree with beautiful lavender leaves. I snapped a few pictures to remember the beauty of this tree and to share it with my children. When we returned home, I was shocked to see the very same trees not only grow on the university campus where I have been teaching for twenty-five years, but also in the neighborhood where we have lived for nearly thirty years! Even though I pass beneath these same trees on my way to and from my daily endeavors, I had never noticed them. Only when travelling, when I had no goal in mind other than to appreciate my surroundings, did I notice something beautiful that had been in plain sight all along, but had eluded me.

Parashat Mas'ei

Seeing the world in a cyclical way is not about being without a destination; rather, the objective is the journey itself. Thus, in our most joyous celebrations, we dance in a circle. At weddings, and on Simchat Torah, we celebrate the circle of Jewish life, enjoying the journey and taking the time to see ourselves as part of that circle. Our sages explain that in the messianic future, the righteous will dance in a circle, and God Himself will stand at its center. Only then will we fully understand that the ultimate destination was the circle itself, and God is, and has always been, right there in the center, in our midst, all along.

Likewise, the weekly cycle that culminates in Shabbat is not meant to be destination-oriented. We are not meant to disregard the six days of the week that lead to Shabbat. Our goal should also include the six days between one Shabbat and the next, by allowing what we have gained on the seventh day—spiritually, emotionally, communally, intellectually—to energize and uplift each subsequent day of the week. By allowing some of the holiness of the Sabbath to "spill over" into our weekday consciousness, we begin to enjoy not only the destination—the holiness of Shabbat—but also the journey through our week that takes us there.

The story of the Israelites' travels in the desert is the story of a nation that was not yet ready to enter the Promised Land. The forty-year delay was not simply a punishment. In order to be worthy of the Land of Israel, the Israelites had to experience a journey that would help them grow, help them achieve spiritual and national maturity. They needed the time and space to achieve new modes of thinking and new modes of experience. Circling the desert was a wonderful introduction to the cyclical experience of the Jewish calendar and Jewish history. It afforded an opportunity to do more than simply arrive at the destination; it taught them to see and appreciate the trees along the way.

ספר
דברים

Parashat Devarim – Tisha B'av
The Price of Hatred

It is often quoted in the name of Rabbi Abraham Isaac Kook that just as the Temple was destroyed due to baseless hatred, it will be rebuilt due to baseless love. While this teaching sounds simple, it is in fact highly nuanced, and deserves more serious consideration.

The image that comes to mind when we hear the words "baseless hatred" is usually one of rampant, wanton violence, yet the precise definition of the Hebrew phrase *sin'at hinam* leads us in a different direction altogether. The word *hinam* is more accurately translated as "free of charge" or "at no cost" in a monetary sense. Rather than hatred for no reason whatsoever, it implies hatred for which the price is somehow incongruous or out of balance. The problem is not that we dislike people for no reason; generally, we all feel we have very good reasons to dislike the people we do. We may have been hurt, insulted, or, worst of all, ignored, and we develop a healthy animus toward the offender as we defend ourselves and our tattered egos. The problem is that more often than not, our response is not proportional: We "overcharge" for these real or perceived wrongs. The price is not right; we pay back with interest, and, as we all know, the Torah prohibits usury.

If we were to be honest with ourselves, we would be forced to recognize that at times the other person had no intention to hurt. Our own insecurity and emotional fragility lead us to interpret the behavior or speech of others as malicious, even when no such malice was intended.

Here, then, is the dilemma: When Rav Kook's teaching is understood as an admonishment against baseless hatred, most of us can, with absolute honesty, categorically state that we are innocent. On the other hand, when we reframe the question and ask instead if we have ever overreacted, if we are guilty of exaggerated responses to real or perceived slights, I am afraid that many of us can answer in the affirmative. We are, in fact, quite guilty, but we are blind to our own malevolence, simply because we think the other person has earned every bit of it. Whatever hatred we have for them is not "free."

As far as the "baseless love" (and not "free love," which conjures up a completely different set of issues), Rav Kook taught us to love others even though they are undeserving. But is this the case? Are we not commanded to love our neighbors as ourselves? Our love for others is not "free" or baseless; it is grounded in the knowledge that every person is created in the image of God, and every Jew is a unique part of our collective, a beautiful piece in the mosaic of our peoplehood. By what right do we imagine that the love and support we should be giving is unwarranted or *free*? This other person is my brother, sister or cousin too-many-times removed. I am obligated by Jewish law to love and care for my Jewish brothers and sisters, to worry about them and constantly consider how I can improve their lives, to pray for each and every other Jew. They are me, and we are one.

And therein lies the rub: We have somehow learned to convince ourselves that the hatred we feel is well-deserved, while the love we are obligated to feel and express is unearned and is given to the undeserving. Undoubtedly, this is what Rav Kook truly intended to convey.

Judaism teaches us to see our world from God's perspective as well as our own. While we justify our hatred of others by focusing on the wrongs they have committed, from God's higher vantage point, our hatred for others is *sinat hinam*— unearned, disproportionate, high-interest payback. While we consider our acts of kindness or gestures of love free and unearned, we are, in fact, fulfilling a very specific obligation to love and care for them.

This dual perspective is discernible in this *parashah*: Moshe recalls the episode of the spies and recounts:

> And you grumbled in your tents, and said, "God brought us out of the land of Egypt because He hated us" (*Devarim* 1:27).

Rashi points out what should be obvious to us: Quite the opposite was the case: "He loved you, but you hated Him."

Here we have the core of *sin'at hinam*—groundless hatred: Lonely, frightened man, controlled by his own insecurity, is unable to feel God's love. In a knee-jerk reaction, he lashes out, with hatred that is both baseless and unearned, projecting this hatred back onto God.

Humankind is a strange species, capable of love yet afraid to love. We fail to consider the true nature of love as our greatest natural resource, which grows exponentially the more it is "used." Why are we so stingy in sharing it with others?

> If we were destroyed, and the world with us, due to baseless hatred, then we shall rebuild ourselves, and the world with us, with baseless love (Rabbi Abraham Isaac Kook, *Orot ha-Kodesh* vol. 3, p. 324).

Yom HaShoah:
Holocaust Remembrance Day
And God Said, "I am Sorry"

Every spring, a number of days of commemoration are observed throughout the Jewish world. Yom HaShoah and Yom HaZikaron, established by the government of Israel, are days in which we honor the memory of the fallen—first for the victims of the Holocaust and then for those who gave their lives to create and defend the State of Israel. On these solemn days, we remember the fallen as individuals, just as we attempt to transmit the lessons learned from tragic loss to the next generation.

Yom HaAtzmaut immediately follows Yom HaZikaron, marking the establishment of the State of Israel and celebrating our continued freedom and sovereignty in our homeland.

These three days, clustered together in a very intensive sequence, create a period of national introspection and stock-taking in which we consider, on the one hand, our many achievements and the unprecedented success of the Jewish nation-state, while on the other hand, the extreme sacrifices that were made to achieve our freedom. By creating the juxtaposition between Remembrance Day and Independence Day, this was the underlying message Israel's founders hoped to convey—a lesson they apparently learned from the fact that the holiday of Purim immediate follows the Fast of Esther: Our victory, our survival, was made possible by almost-unthinkable sacrifice.

Similarly, the darkness of the Holocaust is contrasted with the dawn of the emerging Jewish state—not to insinuate a correlation or "barter" of six million souls for the establishment of the State, but to help us appreciate the contrast between these two eras by observing them on consecutive days. The Holocaust and the creation of the State of Israel should be seen as polar opposites—not only in the political or physical sense, but also, as Rabbi Soloveitchik encouraged us to understand them, in terms of their theological implications.

The Holocaust is an archetypical example of darkness, of the *hester panim* (literally, "hidden face"), based on the verse, "I will surely hide my face on that day" (*Devarim* 31:18). Conversely, the establishment of the modern State of Israel is a revelation of God's presence and active involvement in Jewish history, a dazzling *gillui panim* (revelation) in which God's hand is unmistakable. The contrast between the darkness that we experienced and the emergence into the light and warmth of modern Israel is almost startling.

In a very real sense, the relationship between God and the Jewish people may be likened to the cycle of the moon, which disappears and then reappears, at first as a sliver, and eventually as a full moon. A brief rabbinic comment regarding the new moon may help us reframe this strange shift from darkness to light from a theocentric perspective: On each holiday, we are commanded to bring a sin-offering, just as a sin-offering is brought on the eve of every new month. However, the biblical passage that describes the sin-offering on Rosh Hodesh (the new moon) differs from all the others. In all other instances, the Torah refers simply to the "sin-offering." Only the sacrifice brought on Rosh Hodesh is described as "a sin-offering for God" (*B'midbar* 28:15). The Talmud (*Hullin* 60b) offers a philosophical explanation for this anomaly: God asks that a sin-offering be brought each month to atone for His own sin—the sin of diminishing the moon.

The implications of this teaching are extraordinary, and they speak to the very core of our reality. The world was created with a delicate balance between light and darkness, between clarity and obscurity, between revelation and *hester panim*. Presumably, this balance is necessary in order to create an atmosphere in which man can retain free will, which is the very foundation of our independent existence. In a world in which God's constant, active involvement in human history is always apparent, free will is eclipsed, and man cannot thrive. Ultimately, the periods of darkness, the terrible bouts of existential loneliness, are as spiritually beneficial for us as the periods of light. The waves of *hester panim*, as they are juxtaposed with *gillui panim*, sharpen our awareness of the Divine and encourage us to seek out the spiritual message contained in the darkness, in the silence, in the pain that precedes the appearance of that sliver of moon. It is the struggle with the darkness that allows us to grow.

And yet, God expresses remorse for inflicting upon us the hours, days, even years of darkness and doubt. God takes responsibility for the pain we must experience. "Pray for Me," He says. "Bring an offering to atone for My sin. Forgive Me."

By commanding us to bring this offering, God says, "Forgive Me for the pain you have experienced." We might consider this the flip-side of the coin of the human condition: We all, unavoidably, sin. When we do, we turn to God, we desperately pray and plead for forgiveness. Once each month, the proverbial shoe is on the other foot, and God seeks our forgiveness for the pain inherent in the human condition. Can we rejoice in the loving reunion that ensues as the light overcomes the darkness and we realize that the pain was an indispensable stage in our spiritual growth? Do we have the moral fortitude to forgive God?

Parashat VaEtchanan
Is "One" a Number?

To a large extent, the Book of *Devarim* is a polemic against idolatry. Moshe instructs, cajoles and admonishes as he attempts to inspire the people to follow one God. In *Parashat VaEtchanan* especially, there is a positive declaration, which is often described as the credo of Judaism: "Hear O Israel: God is our Lord, God is One." In this same *parashah,* we find a negative formulation of this same principle: "for God is the Lord and there is no other aside from Him." Both statements seem to teach the same idea: monotheism, belief in one God. There are, however, some nuances that should not go unexamined.

Rabbi Soloveitchik offered an interpretation of the *Shema* that may otherwise have been missed: The word *ehad*, which is usually rendered "one," should in this case be understood as "unique."[41] The distinction is not simply a question of mathematics; it is not that we differ from others in that we limit the number of our deities. This concise statement of our faith does not simply compare Judaism's belief in "only" one God with the dualism or polytheism of other belief systems. According to this view, the declaration, "Hear O Israel, God is our Lord, God is unique" has implications for the nature of that One God: The Deity is completely different, unquantifiable; God alone is *sui generis*, singular and unparalleled. This is our God: The One who creates and sustains the universe is not

41. In a lecture delivered on October 26, 1976.

simply quantitatively different from polytheistic deities, but qualitatively different as well.

What is the nature of this uniqueness? By definition, to create the universe means to exist outside of creation. This universe and all that it contains were created; not so the Being who created it all. The Creator transcends time, space and matter, and is not subject to any of the laws of physics.

This basic, irrefutable principle of Judaism leads to the second statement, "There is no other aside from Him." At first glance, these two statements appear to teach the same idea, albeit in inverse formulations: There is but one God. All other forces or powers are not merely impotent, they are nonexistent. However, the kabbalists delve deeper into the significance of this seemingly redundant declaration. They understand the second statement to mean, "There is nothing other than Him" (*Devarim* 4:35). This kabbalistic insight may be expressed as a mathematical challenge: How is the creation of a finite universe possible, when the starting point is an infinite God? Simply put, adding a finite number to an infinite one will always yield infinity. One cannot add to infinity; the sum total always remains infinite. How, then, is our existence possible alongside an Infinite God?

This three-word phrase *ein od milvado* ("There is nothing other than Him") is actually a profound philosophical and existential statement: There is nothing outside of God. Nothing else truly exists. Reality is God; God is the only reality. While we may "see" many false gods, sense and experience many illusionary realities, there is in fact only one reality—the infinite God who cleared away a small corner of His infinite existence in order to allow our finite universe to coexist. Everything that exists within the finite universe does so at the will of the Infinite God. Should He cease to allow this to be so, our finite universe would be subsumed into God's infinite reality.

The Jewish formulation is not that every aspect of creation *is* God; rather that God sustains every aspect of creation, allowing its coexistence with infinity. We can, indeed, perceive God in all of creation, but we, unlike pantheists or polytheists, understand that what we are in fact perceiving is an expression of God's will, and not some other life force.

For the believer, the existence beyond our own—that existence in which God does not limit Himself for our benefit—is the place of reality. It is infinite and unchanging; it is eternal and permanent. Our finite, fleeting existence is a mere echo of that reality. However, we have been given certain tools that allow us to access that reality: Torah study allows us to observe our own existence from the perspective of the Infinite. Observance of the commandments allows us to develop our relationship with God and to connect with reality. The Torah allows us to perceive God's will, to hear God's voice, as it were. Prayer allows us to approach and speak to God, constituting the second side of the dialogue between God and man. Leading a life of holiness, individually and as a community, allows us to become a part of that other, infinite existence that we call eternity.

When man was first created and placed in Eden, the sense and spirit of the infinite which hovered in the Garden was more immediate and accessible. Our quest, ever since then, has been to seek the road back to Eden and to that experience of the Omnipresent God. Man's search for God is the search for reality; nothing in our physical universe is as real as the relationship with God.

When we say *Shema* we recognize that God is, was, and will be; God is infinite. Saying the *Shema* connects us with infinity, with a reality that is so much greater than our human existence that we close and cover our eyes, averting our gaze from an experience that is so intense and intimate. Precisely because the *Shema* connects us with the infinite nature of God Himself, it has been uttered by millions of Jewish martyrs throughout history.

When we declare *ein od milvado*—there is none/nothing other than God—we recognize that God is reality. God allows us, despite our limitations and shortcomings, to coexist with His infinite and perfect existence. Only when we emulate and imitate His willingness to coexist with others in an imperfect world do we come closer to God. This is how we can bring a touch of infinity into our lives. This is how we "get real."

Parashat Ekev
With All Your Hearts
and All Your Souls

All over the world, every day, for millennia, Jews recite the three chapters of the *Shema*. The first chapter is found in *Parashat VaEtchanan*, last week's Torah reading. The second chapter is found in *Parashat Ekev*.

At first glance, there seems to be quite a bit of repetition between the chapters. For example, the first chapter instructs us to "love God with all your hearts and with all your souls and with all of your resources." The second chapter repeats this instruction, "Love God with all your hearts and all your souls." This apparent repetition suffers from a glaring omission: The obligation to love God with all of our available resources (often understood as monetary resources, possessions) is missing in the second chapter.

This problem is exacerbated by translation into English; in Hebrew, the difference between the two chapters is more apparent, and this is the key to understanding the omission.

The first chapter is stated in the singular and speaks to the individual, while the second chapter speaks in the plural, and addresses the collective.

What emerges from this observation is that the individual is bidden to love God with all of his or her resources, while the community does not have this obligation.

This distinction and its implications are closely related to the well known yet often misunderstood concept of *tikkun olam*—"fixing the world."

The Mishnah in *Sanhedrin* (37a) teaches that whoever saves one life saves an entire world. In Judaism's value system, every life is of infinite value. Nonetheless, the Mishnah in *Gittin* teaches that when redeeming captives, one should not "overpay":

Captives should not be redeemed for more than their value, because of *tikkun olam* (*Gittin* 45a).

Prima facie, this seems to be a very strange application of *tikkun olam,* which many people associate with the "warm and fuzzy" side of Judaism, the Jewish impulse to make the world a better place. In this case, the very same sages who invoke the sanctity of life and the duty to uplift the world, put a price, a monetary value, on the life of a captive. By introducing such pedestrian concerns into the equation, they tacitly condemn the captive to death if the price for release is deemed too high!

The picture comes into sharper focus if we understand the concept of *tikkun olam* in this instance as an expression of macro-economic considerations. Apparently, the halakhic constraints that bind the community differ from those that bind the individual. Even something of infinite value has a price, and that price can be tangible, finite. Had this not been the case, the community as a whole would be obligated to spend all of its collective resources to save one life. And as cruel as it may sound, this would be devastating as a long-term strategy for any community.

Here, then, lies the reason for the glaring omission we noticed in the second chapter of the *Shema*: When the community is addressed, "all your resources" is missing. Communal resources are to be used for the betterment and preservation of the community as a whole, according to the wisdom and the conscience of its leaders. Pragmatism, a word (unfortunately) not usually associated with religion, is a positive guiding force, an overriding consideration in the calculus of resource allocation.

Judaism is a religion of myriad obligations. One of the messages of the second chapter of the *Shema* is another obligation: Simply put, we are obligated as a community to be responsible, to behave in a logical and pragmatic fashion, to spend our communal resources with sensitivity and reason. That is the true meaning of *tikkun olam*.

Parashat Re'eh
Choices

God gives man choices; these are described as blessings and curses, or life and death. Remarkably, mankind has always needed to be encouraged to choose life. This seemingly automatic, rational choice has never been the "no-brainer" it should be. Why would any sane person choose a cursed path that leads to certain death over the blessed path of life? Apparently, the choice is somewhat more complicated, and our judgment curiously clouded. From time immemorial, the Tree of Death and its luscious fruit looked like the gleaming and attractive choice—more delicious, more desirable. In addition, a seductive, serpentine salesman hissed in our ears about how the fruit of this tree could solve all our problems, enlighten and empower us.

Those of you who rushed to consult your Bibles because you do not recall reading about a "tree of death" are partially correct: There was, indeed, a tree of death, presented by God Himself as the antithesis of the Tree of Life. Clearly, in order to allow man to make a choice between these two options, this tree needed a more palatable image, and so it was marketed and promoted as a "Tree of Knowledge of Good and Evil." While many of us often think of this tree and its fruit as a viable option to the other choice, and conveniently refer to it in shorthand as a tree of knowledge, it was, in fact, the tree that represented a confusion of good and evil, a tree whose fruit distanced us from the source of life itself—clarity and understanding, proximity to God and holiness. This tree and its fruit are the physical representation of the choices that lead to death—of experience without understanding, of knowledge without wisdom, of information devoid of values.

This choice, this path in life, has not changed much since the days of Adam and Eve: Even today, in the information age, the toxic cloud of confusion created by the amalgamation of good and evil casts a massive shadow that obscures our sightline to true knowledge and real life. Contemporary examples abound: In our generation, computer technology and the internet give us access to information in staggering quantity, but good and evil are often combined and confused. Is all the information we access reliable? Do we want our children to take in everything the internet has to offer? Can we ourselves, as intelligent and discerning adults, accurately evaluate or adequately assimilate all of the words and images we are fed? Is it any wonder that one of the most successful computer companies in the world (the creator and manufacturer of the machine on which I am writing these words) represents itself by a fruit with a bite missing—perhaps depicting the forbidden fruit?

What the Torah teaches us is not that the internet, or any technology, is evil or forbidden. The image of the Tree of Knowledge of Good and Evil represents the confusion that is to be found in many different aspects of human life. We are warned that the source of truth—absolute truth—is accessible to us, but the fruits of the tree of death continue to entice and attract our attention and imagination. Why are we attracted to this fruit? Are we hard-wired to self-destruct? Were we created with a death wish? Is the urge to experience the fruit of the "tree of death" an attempt to anesthetize ourselves, to punish ourselves, or do we simply desire what we cannot have? Do we fancy ourselves to be gods? Perhaps all of these motives combine; perhaps the confusion of motives is one more result of having ingested, of continuing to ingest, the fruit of the tree that confuses and clouds truth and reality, and leads us astray from our life-source, to death.

As mankind becomes more and more sophisticated, as we obtain and attempt to synthesize more and more information, our need for clarity becomes more and more acute. All of our sophistication has not made us immune to confusion; in fact, we may say that the opposite is true. Now more than ever, we need a healthy dose of the fruit of the Tree of Life—of clear morals and values that can equip us to make sense of the glut of information that is the defining trait of modern life. Our choices often seem so much less cut-and-dried than they were in the Garden of Eden; our lives seem to be composed of so many shades of grey. Moshe's message is that complex moral dilemmas can be distilled into one question: Which choice will lead me closer to my spiritual source of life? Torah—the Tree of Life, with its immutable moral guidelines—provides this clarity. From the dawn of creation, evil has been dressing up, making promises. To choose life, we must focus on the word of God and not the slick salesman selling snake oil; his promises are empty, and the potion never works.

The choice that confronts the People of Israel as they prepare to enter the Promised Land is the choice that confronts us, individually and collectively, to this very day. Once again, two paths diverge from the junction at which we are poised. Will we repeat the mistakes of the past? Will we, once again, choose death? Moshe reminds them, and us, of the choices, and of our capabilities. He calls upon them, as he calls upon us, to rise to the occasion, to raise our heads above the cloud of confusion and not to lose sight of the Tree of Life, the moral compass with which we have been armed. Above all, Moshe reminds us that we are capable of making the right choice—but it is a choice. God, for His part, is rooting for us: "Choose life."

Parashat Shoftim
The Vagabond

A dark, lonely road; swift movements, footsteps, a thud, silence; a corpse....

Who was he? Presumably, the kind of person who is alone in the dark of night, the type of person who wanders from town to town, the type of person who does not really have a place he calls home; a vagabond.

His death may not necessarily be mourned. His friends and family have lost track of him, and he has been swallowed by anonymity. When people do see him, they avert their eyes. He reminds them of something they would rather not see: The human condition in a particularly compromised form. He reminds them of their own vulnerability. Most prefer not to look; some throw him a few coins and turn away feeling better about themselves. They move on, to their warm homes, to their loved ones. He, too, moves on—to harm's way and the dangers of the street and the night.

It is easy to move on; we have almost no choice. We try to forget, until we hear about a victim. We are forced to face the knowledge that this corpse was once a human being, like ourselves, with the breath of God pulsating in his lungs. This man was a son of Adam, and like Abel, he was also lured by his brother out of the city to a field—and to his death. "The sound of your brother's blood cries out to Me from the ground," God admonished Cain—and all of us. The nameless corpse cannot be disregarded; this crime cannot be ignored. The question is, do we hear this blood crying out? And if we do, isn't it really too little, too late? Did we do everything we could to avoid this tragedy? Did we care for this stranger as we should have? Did we invite him to our homes? Did we find him a job? Did we try to help him heal his tattered life, or did his tattered clothes scare us? Did we simply turn away?

The Torah addresses the question of accountability in such cases through a rather elaborate ritual, a demonstrative process that is meant to be both educational and, it is hoped, transformative: The distance from the scene of the crime is carefully measured by rope, and the nearest town is accused of indifference, of criminal negligence that borders on complicity. Indifference contributed to this tragedy, and the town's elders must wash their hands and declare their innocence—if their conscience allows it. Maybe this will prevent the next murder.

In this *parashah*, the Torah discusses the large, important institutions of public life, and the individual may be easily forgotten. *Parashat Shoftim* establishes the framework of the Jewish polis: The judiciary system and police force, the powers and limitations of kings and prophets. The inclusion of the guidelines for cases such as that of our vagabond specifically in this context teaches us a powerful underlying principle: The singular purpose of all of the instruments of power is to protect the individual, especially the weakest, most anonymous members of society. If we do not protect the weak and vulnerable, what type of society have we created? The king and all of his horses and all of his men are not merely symbols of civic or national pride. Their purpose is to protect the people, to create "top-down" morality. This is their mandate, their *raison d'être*. This same *parashah* commands the kings of Israel to keep their true purpose in their sights at all times: The king must carry the Torah is in his heart and his arms. The Torah puts clear limits on pomp and circumstance, protocol and ceremony. Responsibilities far outweigh the privileges of Jewish kings and leaders.

For many people, the essence of Judaism is its moral teachings; for others, ritual seems more important. I once heard my teacher, Rabbi Yosef Dov Soloveitchik,[42] illustrate the Jewish concept of the balance between these two aspects: It is well-known that *kohanim* are commanded to avoid contact with the impurity of death. They do not attend funerals or visit cemeteries, except for their closest family members. The *Kohen Gadol* may not defile himself even for those closest to him. However, the Talmud teaches that when the High Priest comes upon a corpse out in the fields, he is commanded to personally bring the body to burial. Even on the eve of Yom Kippur, when the hopes and spiritual aspirations of the entire nation are all focused on him and channeled through him, if he happens upon the corpse of a lowly, anonymous vagabond, the *Kohen Gadol* must defile himself, pick up the body and physically bring the person to a dignified burial. In what he admitted was an embellishment of the talmudic passage, Rabbi Soloveitchik illuminated this basic principle of Judaism: The dignity of a man who may have been scorned, a man who no longer feels any pain, takes precedence over the most important participant in the most spiritually charged scene of the year, the Yom Kippur service. Human dignity trumps ritual. The nameless hobo is more important than the High Priest. This is the great humanism that lies at Judaism's core, and the Torah does not allow us to forget it. For if we look away, if we push the vagabond just beyond the verge of our peripheral vision and avoid thinking about the needs of the anonymous person on the margins of society, swift movements, footsteps, a thud, silence. A corpse.

---

42. In a lecture delivered January 3, 1958.

Parashat Ki Tetzei
Abuse

Parashat Ki Tetzei discusses a host of abusive behaviors, some sexual and others financial. In general, the Torah legislates against these aberrant behaviors, deeming them illegal. We have no difficulty understanding these laws; as a whole, the objective of Torah law is to create a just, healthy society. Abusive behavior of any kind runs counter to this objective.

We are all too familiar with the various outcomes of abuse: The abuser's compassion becomes dulled and often a downward spiral of self-loathing ensues. As for the victim, abuse often breeds abuse: The victim becomes oppressor, perpetuating the cycle, or internalizes the abuse and suffers the destruction of self-esteem that leads to depression or self-abuse.

Oddly, one case seems to break the rule. In the strange and disturbing instance of the female captive taken in battle, the Torah seems to allow abusive behavior rather than legislating against it. The text does not mince words; this is labeled as abusive behavior, but instead of legislating against "having one's way" with a woman taken against her will in a time of war, the Torah allows it—but adds one major caveat: Your captive will become your spouse. It seems that legislation in this case is aimed at limiting the abuse, not preventing it.

The talmudic discussion of this topic attempts to frame and clarify the law, labeling it a concession to the evil inclination.[43]

43. Talmud Bavli *Kiddushin* 21b.

This "clarification" actually makes things even more disturbing: If the sages understood that the desire to take this woman is evil, should it not have been prohibited, like so many other expressions of man's baser urges and instincts?

In the charged atmosphere of the battlefield, the normal standards of decency seem to be suspended: Behaviors even young children know are prohibited—taking things that belong to someone else, using force to the point of violence, even taking lives—become the order of the day. In circumstances such as these, the women on the enemy's side become vulnerable; they, too, are most likely a part of the war effort, either actively engaged or as the support system for the enemy's forces. Be that as it may, the Torah points out that abusive behavior—even towards this sort of enemy—is not without consequences: A woman taken captive in a time of war becomes a wife, and enjoys all the rights and privileges afforded by Torah law. Should her captor-turned-husband subsequently choose to send her away, she is not to be discarded or abandoned. She is not chattel; she is a free human being.

And yet, although this is certainly a far cry from the treatment of captives common to other societies and cultures in antiquity, the knowledge that the Torah is somewhat more "enlightened" is not entirely satisfying (at least not to modern sensibilities). In fact, the sages of the Talmud themselves seemed unsatisfied, and added one further point to consider: Following the discussion of the captive/wife, the Torah discusses the rebellious son. The lesson, then, is that the product of this strange and troubled union is destined to be problematic. An abusive relationship cannot beget healthy offspring. The damage goes far beyond the two people directly involved; spousal abuse destroys the children, as well.[44]

44. Talmud Bavli *Sanhedrin* 107b. See Rashi, *Devarim* 21:11.

The talmudic discussion is intended to set off alarm bells: Abuse spawns a cycle of abuse. Violence begets violence; poor impulse control breeds another generation of poor impulse control. When passions are unchecked, when the need for instant gratification is allowed to override reason and prudence, when a person looks no further than the present moment, the consequences can be enormous.

This section of the Torah challenges us to consider the eventual outcome of one act of passion left untamed. Perhaps the sages of the Talmud hoped that pointing out the consequences would help potential abusers muster the strength to bridle their impulses: Consider, they tell us, the effect your actions will have on your unborn children and grandchildren.

In this context, we may take a more nuanced approach to the closing section of the *parashah*, the call to wage war on Amalek. This nation "abused" the People of Israel on the road when we left Egypt, when we were spiritually and physically vulnerable. On a certain level, the imperative to destroy Amalek is a call to eradicate the very source of abusive behavior.

In concluding the *parashah* on this note, the Torah imparts a message that is both therapeutic and practical: Cycles can be broken. Abusive behavior need not be passed down inexorably from abuser to victim. The lessons of abuse can be learned; rather than creating a new generation of abusers, it can breed sensitive, empathetic souls. Pain is only irredeemable if it is random and meaningless. When we learn through our pain, we can banish the vicious cycle of abuse and replace it with kindness.

This is one of the most often-repeated imperatives in the Torah, especially in this particular *parashah*: Over and over, we are reminded that we, as individuals, as a family, as a nation, have known all too well what it is to be abused. We were slaves, we were downtrodden and abused, and we are therefore expected to have learned the lessons of that pain, and to live to a higher standard. Abuse transformed into kindness: This, indeed, is the cornerstone of an enlightened, just society.

Parashat Ki Tavo
A Recipe for Happiness

Modern man is many things, but more than anything else, modern man is privileged. Had previous generations caught a glimpse of our lives they would have been in awe, convinced that we live in utopia. So much of the drudgework that constituted the majority of daily life in antiquity, the menial labor that made subsistence possible, has been conquered by automation. The convenience and luxury of modern life, which we often take for granted, transcend the imagination of the great thinkers of the past and put the wildest dreams of the wealthy and powerful of yesteryear to shame.

And yet, with all of this technology, with all of the ease and comfort, modern man is not happy. Are ad agencies and large corporations solely to blame? Can we attribute depression, anxiety and disfunctionality to the billions of dollars they spend each year to make us constantly aware that we do not yet own the newest, sleekest, smallest (or largest), most powerful model? Can our malaise be merely the product of envy, or is something else missing?

To a large extent, *Parashat Ki Tavo* deals with happiness. The opening paragraphs command the farmer, who has worked hard all year, to bring his first fruits to Jerusalem and express his thanks to God for this bounty. The prayer of thanksgiving is woven together with a brief re-telling of our national history: We recall our national origins, the period of slavery, the years of wandering and homelessness. We recall a time and place when we were threatened, when our very survival was uncertain. This display of historical consciousness is designed to give context to our current success. Our hard work has paid off, but it was built on the experiences of the past; moreover, when contrasted with the hopelessness of the past, our current success is that much sweeter.

There is, however, another aspect to the rite of the first fruits: We are commanded to thank God for His gifts, thus recognizing a type of partnership with God. Our material success is not ours alone; it is not only our hard work and our national or historical consciousness that has allowed us to achieve. Just as we are not alone when our prospects seem bleak, so too we are not alone when we succeed, through the sweat of our brow, to build and innovate, sow and reap, invent and improve our lives.

Modern man, intoxicated with his own success, is prone to hubris. He sees himself as a self-made man, and worships his creator every time he glances in the mirror. But tragically, despite all of his achievements, modern man quite often feels very much alone. Although we have at our disposal almost inconceivable tools of communication, we have lost touch with our selves. We have forgotten how to speak honestly with ourselves, and how to speak to God. The barrage of communication and information all but drowns out the sound of our inner voice, and we fall out of touch; authentic prayer is dismissed as a quaint, abandoned tradition from the past.

Like Narcissus gazing into the water while perched on a rock, modern man no longer recalls where he came from, and his own self-absorption mesmerizes him. He is isolated, and because he has forgotten the past, he has no humility, no perspective, no context. At the same time, he jeopardizes his connection with the future: Only when we transmit historical consciousness to our children, and live beyond the narrow confines of the present, do we stand a chance of being appreciated by our children—rather than being rejected, in turn, as a relic from the past.

The Torah gives us a formula to combat narcissism, hubris and the existential loneliness they cause—a recipe for happiness: Keep an eye on the past. Know that you are part of something much greater than yourself—a nation that has arisen through trials and tribulations. Remember where we come from. Bring God into the celebration of your success; celebrate in front of God and thank God for your good fortune. Share this perspective with your spouse, and with your children. Be generous; share your happiness and the gifts God has given you with those who are less fortunate:

And you shall rejoice in all the good that the Almighty God has given you and your household; you and the Levi, and the stranger in your midst (*Devarim* 22:11).

The recipe for happiness combines all these things: Hard work to keep you honest; historical consciousness to provide context for your success; family and community to provide perspective. Healthy communication, generosity and humility will be inevitable dividends.

Parashat Nitzavim-Vayelech
The High Holy Days: Belief in Man

The season of Rosh Hashanah and Yom Kippur fills our minds and hearts with so many thoughts and emotions that go beyond our normal framework. This unique time of the Jewish year stands in stark contrast to the New Year's experience marked by the Gregorian calendar: The approach to Rosh Hashanah is counted down by a month of prayer, introspection and rapprochement, while the approach to the secular new year is marked off in shopping days. Rosh Hashanah is steeped in awe and reverence; more often than not, secular new year's day is characterized by the hangover left from a night of revelry. Throughout the ages and in every corner of the globe, Jews gather in synagogues to hear the shofar, not in Times Square; we kiss the Torah, and not the somewhat inebriated person who happens to be standing nearby.

Yet while our mood is more somber, our thoughts more serious, our holiday season has a festive, even celebratory element as well. This is the frame of mind that envelops us as we connect to holiness and re-discover the purity of our souls. In common with the secular celebration of the new year, we, too, make "new year's resolutions," although our aspirations are of a higher order and, it is hoped, our resolve greater and our follow-through more successful. Judaism instructs us to use this time to shine a spotlight on our lives and lifestyles. With great thought, soul searching and angst, we strip off the veneer and examine the core of our existence. We are given the opportunity to set aside this time to ask the great existential questions: Who am I? Who do I wish to be? Have I made the wrong choices? Am I falling short? What do I need to change?

This process is called *teshuvah*. To better understand the concept of *teshuvah*, we may view it through the prism of concepts taken from our own frame of reference. One approach is to consider our personal "balance sheet"; the traditional term for this approach is *heshbon ha-nefesh*, a very personal calculation that allows us to measure the spiritual assets and liabilities accumulated over the course of our daily lives. The process of *teshuvah* allows us to restructure—that is, to convert debt into equity, either through repentance and/or by taking decisions and actions to increase our assets. This is the "recovery plan" at the core of the High Holy Days: *Teshuvah, tefillah* (prayer) and *tzedakah* (acts of charity) turn us back from the brink of spiritual bankruptcy and dissolution.

The scriptural source for the concept of *teshuvah* is found in *Parashat Nitzavim*, read every year just before Rosh Hashanah:

> And you will return to God your Lord, and you will obey Him, doing everything that I am commanding you today. You and your children [will repent] with all your heart and with all your soul (*Devarim* 30:2).

The verse seems quite clear, yet rabbinic authorities differ in their understanding of its implications. Some of the sages read this verse as a commandment, requiring every Jew to undergo the process of *teshuvah* we have described. This approach focuses on the first word of the verse, *veshavta*, "and you will return," and disregards the larger narrative context in which it appears. Other rabbinic authorities, reading the verse in context, understand it as a description of a time in the future when terrible things befall the Jewish people, and they return to God.

In this vein, we find an intriguing formulation in the writings of Maimonides. While apparently sidestepping the debate regarding *teshuvah* as a commandment, Maimonides' thoughts on this verse may be an even more powerful statement:

> The Torah has already promised that, ultimately, Israel will repent towards the end of the exile, and will be redeemed immediately, as stated [in the verse]: "There shall come a time when [you will experience] all these things... and you will return to God, your Lord..." (Maimonides, *Hilkhot Teshuvah* 7:5).

For Maimonides, *teshuvah* is not just a good idea and sound spiritual accounting; it is the destiny of the Jewish People. This is our future, a glorious national renaissance in which the individuals that comprise the Jewish nation move closer to God and mend their ways. It is the culmination of our history, the light at the end of the tunnel of millennia of suffering and existential struggle.

In a sense, the belief in this glorious future is in actuality a belief in the Jewish People. It is a belief that, as a collective, we have the spiritual sensitivity, intelligence, fortitude and acumen to make the right decisions. It is the belief that each and every Jew has the power to move the nation as a whole in a positive direction. With this understanding, debating whether or not *teshuvah* is a commandment becomes irrelevant; in this time of heightened awareness, people will undergo the process of repentance solely because it is sound spiritual advice. Whether or not it is required of us, we will be eager to fix the past and recalibrate our souls. We will not need to be commanded to take advantage of an opportunity for our debts to be erased, our spiritual books to be balanced.

Following Maimonides' formulation, the gathering of Jews in synagogues on the High Holy Days may be seen as a microcosm of the messianic age. When houses of prayer fill to capacity, when we feel the unprecedented pull of Jewish souls gravitating towards God, there is more than just guilt at play. This is the fulfillment of the prophecy contained in the verse in *Parashat Nitzavim*, the expression of the great spiritual renaissance that is part and parcel of Jewish destiny.

May the holiday season be a harbinger of the messianic age, releasing us all from our spiritual debts and uplifting us to the great spiritual heights of which we are capable.

Rosh Hashanah
A Holy Family

On Rosh Hashanah, lowly man is called upon to participate in the coronation of the King of Kings, God Almighty. The very fact that we are permitted to participate in this momentous event uplifts us and gives us a sense of significance and purpose which, it is hoped, will propel us to new spiritual heights. As we recognize God's dominion over us, we are called upon to live up to the capabilities with which we are endowed, by virtue of the image of God within each and every one of us. Nonetheless, at the end of the day, we are but servants of God. Despite the aura of importance Rosh Hashanah gives us, the chasm between man and God remains unfathomable and unchanging. Although we participate in the coronation, we are so far beneath the King that our declarations almost seem absurd.

This coronation ceremony reaches its climax as we blow the shofar. At that moment, we declare and accept God's kingship. How strange, then, is the prayer we utter at that very moment, as the echo of the shofar blast hangs in the air:

Today is the birthday of the world. Today all creatures of the world are judged, whether as children or as servants. If as children, be merciful with us as a father has mercy on his children. If as servants, we beseech You with our eyes, until You will be gracious to us and bring to light our verdict, O awesome and holy God.

Rather than accepting our lot as servants of God, we entertain the possibility that we might enjoy a special relationship with the Almighty. The same idea is articulated in another central prayer of the Days of Awe, *Avinu Malkenu* ("Our Father, Our King"). We know—cognitively, logically—that we are but servants, yet we beseech God to think of us as His children. We pray, even beg, for God to relate to us as a loving, nurturing, forgiving parent, and not as the master of undeserving slaves.

The difference between these two relationships is far-reaching, because the nature of our relationship with God lies at the very heart of our religious life and informs every aspect of our personal and national existence. This is best illustrated by a debate, recorded in the Talmud, between the great Rabbi Akiva and a Roman dignitary.

> This question was actually put by Turnus Rufus to R. Akiva: "If your God loves the poor, why does He not support them?" He replied, "So that we may be saved through them from the punishment of Hell." "On the contrary," said the other, "it is this which condemns you to Hell. I will illustrate by a parable. Suppose an earthly king was angry with his servant and put him in prison and ordered that he should be given no food or drink, and a man went and gave him food and drink. If the king heard, would he not be angry with him? And you are called 'servants,' as it is written, 'For unto me the children of Israel are servants'" (*Bava Batra* 10a).

The Roman prefect argued that by helping the poor, man defies God who had sentenced them to a life of poverty.

R. Akiva answered him: "I will illustrate by another parable. Suppose an earthly king was angry with his son, and put him in prison and ordered that no food or drink should be given to him, and someone went and gave him food and drink. If the king heard of it, would he not send him a present? And we are called 'sons,' as it is written, 'You are sons of the Almighty God'" (*Bava Batra* 10a).

The crux of the argument is as follows: Turnus Rufus, the Roman general, saw his servants—and, by extension, all of mankind—in terms of the hierarchy of power. All of us, according to this view, are but servants to the powerful. Rabbi Akiva saw the nature of the relationship between God and man in a completely different light. Rabbi Akiva saw mankind as children of God, not simply as servants.

But what is it that makes us children of God? The answer is as simple as it is profound: *If you want God to treat you as His child, you must treat other people as your brothers and sisters.*

This past year the people of Israel suffered horrific trauma, yet as the news of kidnapping, death and war spread, the response was heroic.[45] Something special happened: An entire nation, a nation not limited by geography, felt as if those three boys were their own sons or brothers. As our soldiers made their way to the border and into Gaza, an entire nation poured out so much love and care and empathy that here in Israel we felt an almost seismic vibration beneath our feet. Our differences melted away; petty political positions seemed trite. For the first time in a long time, we felt that we are truly one people, of one heart. We were able to feel the heartbeat of this beautiful collective. All of

---

45. This essay was written in the aftermath of the kidnapping of the three teenage martyrs in Gush Etzion, and the events which followed.

our hearts skipped a beat when the sirens wailed; all our hearts stopped for a moment with the tragic news that the bodies of the three martyrs were found. All our hearts shrank each time the death of another fallen soldier was announced.

And then there were the acts of kindness, the things that made our hearts swell and come back to life—gestures that seemed to border on the irrational. Gifts, letters of encouragement and gratitude, clothes, food and money came pouring in. Perfect strangers reached out to residents of the south, families hosted those whose homes were threatened, communities looked after the wives and children of the men who went to battle. In fact, none of this was irrational. It all made perfect sense: We felt that our brothers and sisters were in trouble, and when members of our family are vulnerable we step up to protect them. We feel empathy; we help them through times of stress and need. We feel their pain, and we shower them with love. This summer, we reminded ourselves what it means to be a family—a big, raucous, loud, beautiful family, made up of *sabras* (native-born Israelis), *olim* (immigrants) and diaspora Jews, Sefaradim and Ashkenazim, white and black, ultra-Orthodox and secular and everything in between. We were one.

And so, this year, when the shofar sounds, we can stand tall and proud as we coronate God as King as the Universe, and as we recite the prayer afterward, we can say—at least in our hearts: "Treat us as your children. This year, show us compassion, because we behaved like a compassionate, caring family. Show us kindness and love, in the merit of the kindness and love we have shown one another. Behave toward us like a forgiving parent, because we have shown how much we care for our brothers and sisters."

In the merit of everything we experienced together this past summer—the good and the bad, the sacrifice, the unity, the loss and the reaffirmation of commitment—may God write and seal the entire Jewish People in the book of life, and grant us a year of peace, health, happiness, love, prosperity and spiritual enlightenment. May He treat us with love, caring and affection, just as any father would treat their child.

Shana Tova

Parashat Ha'azinu
(Don't) Look Back

We live in the present, fantasize about the future, and distort the past. The mind, mankind's greatest tool, can imagine a beautiful future and set in motion the plan to implement it. Alternatively, man can be weighed down by the past, unable to escape preconceptions, negative experiences, or abuses imagined or real. Both the positive and negative echoes of the past may be exaggerated, distorted, or simply expunged from memory. In fact, it may be impossible to separate fact from interpretation when looking back; our personal memories are often colored by opinion and emotion, and so much of our collective memory has been shaped by the opinions and agendas of historians.

As opposed to previous generations, modern man is far more engrossed by the future than by the past. The past is seen as primitive and depressing, while the future is unlimited, a blank canvas ready to be filled with dazzling colors.

The days leading up to the New Year are an ideal opportunity to consider Judaism's historical consciousness, our relationship with the past and our attitudes toward the future. The Jewish New Year is commonly known as Rosh Hashanah, yet is referred to in the liturgy as Yom HaZikaron, "the Day of Memory," based on a verse in *Vayikra* (23:24). On this day, God remembers our actions; on this day, we recall our own actions, review and reconsider our personal and collective behavior.

A River Flowed from Eden

Fittingly, the *parashah* that is read on the Shabbat closest to Rosh Hashanah charges us to remember the past:

Remember days long gone by. Ponder the years of each generation. Ask your father and let him tell you, and your grandfather, who will explain it (*Devarim* 32:7).

We are enjoined to recall the great contributions of the past, to read the books penned by our ancestors, to open our hearts and minds to receive the orally transmitted wisdom of the ages, to become a living link in the chain of tradition. Indeed, a part of us still lives in the past.

And yet, we have an honest view of the past, not a deconstructionist "nostalgia isn't what it used to be" attitude. Everything that we are taught about the past, from the biblical narrative through modern Jewish history, teaches us to see the roses as well as the thorns. Authentic Jewish scholarship aims to teach us to be inspired by the beauty while at the same time to learn from the mistakes. Unlike revisionist historians, we do not whitewash the past or obscure inconvenient truths. We acknowledge the mistakes, the sins, the lapses in our personal and collective biographies and own up to them.

But Judaism does not stop there. Beyond the realm of historical accuracy and the insight into the human condition that can be gained from the study of history, Judaism's view of history concerns itself with the transcendent: Not only can we learn from the past, not only can we apply the lessons of the past to the future, but through historical consciousness, we can change the past. Thus, during the days leading up to Rosh Hashanah through the end of Yom Kippur the liturgy repeats the seemingly strange formulation: "however we *and our ancestors* have sinned."

Parashat Ha'azinu

The Jewish concept of confession before God is not unfamiliar, yet the additional phrase seems to do no more and no less than malign the dead. What good can come out of slandering our ancestors? Herein lies the key to the concept of *teshuvah*: When we look honestly and sincerely at our own behavior and take responsibility, when we express remorse and make a commitment to change, we take our relationship with God to a higher level than it was even before the sin. The negative behavior becomes the basis of a new, more honest and loving relationship with God. This same dynamic holds true for sins committed by previous generations: When we take an honest look at the negative behaviors of previous generations, when we see ourselves and our lives as part of the dynamic set in motion by those that preceded us, when we take responsibility as a living link in that chain, we can use the mistakes of our ancestors to forge a stronger relationship with God. We can change sins committed in the past to points of departure on a new path toward holiness. Sins of the past are elevated, re-formed.

The greatest expression of man's free will is not simply deciding what we will do as we move from the present toward the future. When we use our newfound understanding to give new meaning to past misdeeds, we re-cast negative behavior and change the past. This is Judaism's true historical consciousness: It is within our power to give form and meaning not only to the present, not only to the future, but to the past as well.

Parashat VeZot HaBrachah
Ending, and Beginning Again

In this *parashah*, we read the closing verses of the Torah:

> There never arose in Israel a prophet like Moshe, who
> knew God face to face. (No one else could produce) the
> signs and miracles that God sent him to perform in the
> land of Egypt, to Pharaoh and all of his land, or any of
> the mighty acts and great sights that Moshe displayed
> before the eyes of all Israel (*Devarim* 34:10-12).

The focus seems to be a "send-off" for Moshe, stressing his
greatness and stature as a prophet and servant of God. However,
the underlying message should not be missed: It was Moshe who
brought the Torah down from heaven, and therefore his status
as prophet is intertwined with the status of the Torah itself.

Interestingly enough, Rashi associates this final phrase of
the Torah with one of the more unorthodox episodes in Moshe's
tenure as the leader of the Israelites. According to Rashi's
understanding of these final verses, Moshe is to be remembered
for posterity for what he did "before all of Israel." And what is it
that Moshe did in such a public and unforgettable way? Surely,
there are many possible answers, many possible candidates
for the most public and unforgettable proof of Moshe's unique
stature as Israel's greatest prophet. And yet, according to Rashi,
this verse is referring specifically to what Moshe did in front of

the "eyes of all of Israel" at the foot of Mount Sinai, and not at its apex: Moshe is remembered for *breaking* the Tablets of the Covenant upon which God Himself had carved the words of the Torah. Is Moshe, then, to be remembered for all time not as the "law-giver" but for being, in an excruciatingly literal sense, the "breaker" of the law? And is this a fitting message for the final verse of the Torah—not the giving of the law but rather the shattering of the law?

There is a rabbinic teaching that may shed light on the underlying message. The Midrash teaches that before God created our world, He "created worlds and destroyed them." This is a remarkably brazen teaching: Surely, the all-powerful and all-knowing God could have created a world that was to His liking the first time around. God has no need for trial-and-error creation, and the Midrash is not to be understood as implying any shortcoming on God's part. Instead, this Midrash contains a profound principle of Jewish philosophy concerning the imperfection inherent in human nature.

The human condition is paradoxical: We are created in the image of God, yet we are, in fact, perfectly imperfect. Man makes mistakes. It is our ability to make choices and err, our ability to recover equilibrium and to learn from our mistakes, that defines us. This, and not merely opposable thumbs, is what sets us apart from the other creatures in our world. Our sages transmitted, through the Midrash, the importance of failed attempts that are used as the building blocks of future success.

Rashi's commentary on the final verses of the Torah expresses the same idea: Moshe ascended Mount Sinai and achieved the highest spiritual level of any human being in history, but he is to be remembered for his response to the failure of his people: He smashed the Tablets, and started again. He worked his way back up the mountain, literally and figuratively, from ground zero.

Rather than eradicating the evidence of failure, the shattered Tablets were housed and guarded in the very same Holy Ark as the second set of Tablets that Moshe brought down to the people. Our eventual success is thus seen as an outgrowth of our previous failures. This is surely an important parting message: The conclusion of the Torah is intertwined with its beginning. We complete the annual cycle of weekly Torah readings and seamlessly begin anew. We start again. We do not allow past failures to discourage us; we continue to strive to understand and fulfill the lessons contained in the Torah, continue to strive to perfect ourselves and our world, even though we have fallen short of the goal before. Just as God did not "despair" of creating humankind despite its failures, just as God "started over," so Moshe is to be remembered for all time as the prophet who smashed the Tablets of the Covenant—but did not despair. He started again, undiscouraged, and led the people to a new beginning.

A perfect God gave a perfect Torah to imperfect man; the result is the imperfection that is "built in" to the very core of the human condition. Yet this imperfect result is not a cross that we bear, an indelible "mark of Cain" or an inescapable and insurmountable state of guilt and inadequacy. The lesson of the final verses of the Torah, like the lesson of the Midrash that paints the backdrop of our world, is that imperfect man is given free will, and when we fall short, when we fail to perfect the world or ourselves, we must start over again. When we reach the end of the Torah, we begin again from *Bereishit*. This is not a sign of failure but an expression of human nature: We are a work in progress.

.

Made in the USA
Charleston, SC
05 April 2016